Estate Settlements

in

Blount County, Tennessee

Naming Heirs Extracted from:

Execution Book II, Chancery Court
February 1872–February 1893;

Execution Book II, County Court
April 1893–February 1915;

and the Workbook of
James A. Greer, Clerk and Master
Chancery Court, 1885–1890

Albert W. Dockter, Jr.

HERITAGE BOOKS
2011

HERITAGE BOOKS

AN IMPRINT OF HERITAGE BOOKS, INC.

Books, CDs, and more—Worldwide

For our listing of thousands of titles see our website
at
www.HeritageBooks.com

Published 2011 by
HERITAGE BOOKS, INC.
Publishing Division
100 Railroad Ave. #104
Westminster, Maryland 21157

Copyright © 1996 Albert W. Dockter, Jr.

Other books by the author:

Blount County, Tennessee Chancery Court Records: Book 0 and Book 1, 1852–1865

Blount County, Tennessee Chancery Court Records: Book 1, Part II, 1866–1869

*Estate Settlements of Blount County, Tennessee, Naming Heirs Extracted from:
Execution Book II, Chancery Court, February 1872–February 1893;
Execution Book II, County Court, April 1893–February 1915;
and the Workbook of James A. Greer, Clerk and Master, Chancery Court, 1885–1890*

Revolutionary War Veteran William Keeble of Blount County, Tennessee and His Heirs

William Keeble of Blount County, Tennessee

International Standard Book Numbers
Paperbound: 978-0-7884-0395-8
Clothbound: 978-0-7884-8699-9

CONTENTS

FOREWORD

This book embodies the contents of three books which are in the Chancery Court storage area at the Blount County, Tennessee Courthouse.

1) A book I call: James A. Greer's Workbook.
2) Chancery Court Execution Book II, February 24, 1872-February 24, 1893.
3) County Court Execution Book II, April 29, 1893-February 1915.

Part 1

It would appear that the Workbook was devised by James A. Greer, Clerk and Master, of the Chancery Court to aid him in receiving funds from the sale of land which was necessitated by the death of the landowner. Equally important to Mr. Greer, and the Court, was the dispersment of the funds held in the Clerk and Masters office, to the heirs.

Each of these settlements was started with a lawsuit heard before the Chancellor. If the Chancellor determined that the land should be sold by Decree of Partition, it was sold, usually to the highest bidder, usually on time, with interest.

In the Workbook the EVEN numbered pages listed the principals in the suit, the date filed, who the land was sold to and for how much. Most of the time the deceased owners name was given. Beneath these facts a list of heirs was given and their proportion of the funds allocated to each of them.

On the ODD numbered pages was the amount dispersed to each heir which was usually accompanied with the signature of the heir.

In some cases the above facts were not recorded on the even numbered pages but were revealed in the heirs' statement of receipt.

I copied the ODD numbered pages only if they revealed some family relationship with the deceased, or completed some fact omitted on the EVEN numbered pages.

The time period of this book appeared to be from 1868 to 1880. You will note that the funds for the last few suits were handled by J.C.M. Bogle, Deputy Clerk. The work ended abruptly with Page #109 and left 200 pages without an entry.

Parts 2 and 3

The word EXECUTION has a sinister connotation to the average layman. However, in legal terminology the word EXECUTION concerns the procedure in concluding a Judgement rendered by a court of law.

The three books included in this work list, for the most part, the living heirs in Estate Settlements and the proportionate share each heir received from that estate.

There are two classes of subjects I deleted from these books.
1) Insolvent Estates. As there were no heirs listed when insolvency occurred those suits were omitted.
2) Bastardy. These suits were instituted to establish paternity and secure financial assistance for the mother, usually.
If one has knowledge of an illegitimate heir in which a lawsuit was filed he or she might find information relative to the parties in the two Execution Docket books here-in.

These three books were the only volumes available in the Chancery Court storage area under this title. One must assume that preceding and succeeding tomes have been moved to another site to make room for more current materials needing storage space. The secondary site is not presently available for research purposes.

It is my thought that these lists of heirs may assist many genealogists in their quest for kin in Blount County, Tennessee.

AWD

WORKBOOK OF JAMES A. GREER,

CLERK AND MASTER OF THE CHANCERY COURT

BLOUNT COUNTY, TENNESSEE

1868-1890

Copied from the original by:

Albert W. Dockter, Jr.

Editor's Note: As related earlier, the only entries omitted were repetitious words on the ODD numbered pages used to prove the heir had been remunerated for his or her share of the estate.

Pg. 1   A.C. HUNTER Vs: THOMAS HUNTER & SAMUEL HUNTER Ptn. to sell land filed Dec. 15, 1868. Land sold May 24, 1869. A.C. HUNTER gdn. for THOMAS A. and SAMUEL M. HUNTER - minors. $239.10 BEN TAYLOR Estate.

Pg. 2   THOMAS VINEYARD Vs: The Heirs of JNO. BREAKBILL, Dec'd. Sept. 21, 1868. Each heir due $136.70
W.T. VINEYARD and wife JAMES CRUISE and wife
JAMES MAYS and wife JOHN CRUISE and wife
ELIZABETH NEWMAN ADAM BREAKBILL
SARAH CUNNINGHAM ALEXANDER LOGAN and wife
JOHN BREAKBILL HENRY BREAKBILL
MARTHA J. BREAKBILL SALINA BREAKBILL
SEREPTA BREAKBILL
JAMES PALMER and wife
PETER BREAKBILL

Pg. 4   JAMES TAYLOR Vs: Heirs at Law of BEN TAYLOR, Dec'd. Nov. 16, 1864. Each heir due $169.33 unless otherwise specified.
SUSAN TAYLOR (BEST), dec'd.
MARY TAYLOR (lives in Missouri)
ELIZABETH TAYLOR (MCMAHON), dec'd. (2 heirs in Texas)

JAMES TAYLOR
WILLIAM TAYLOR
NANCY TAYLOR (BEST)
BEN TAYLOR
ISAAC TAYLOR, dec'd.
MARGARET TAYLOR (CARPENTER, dec'd.)
Heirs of SUSAN TAYLOR BEST are as follows: $24.20 each.
SAM'L B. BEST
CHRIS C. BEST
LOUISA BEST (wife of CHRIS BEST)
NANCY C. BEST (wife of H.H. MORTON)
LUTITIA BEST (wife of M.C. BEST, dec'd.)
ELIZH. A. BEST (wife of D.K. MARTIN) Illinois
MARTHA BEST (wife of WILLIAM SLOAN, dec'd.)
MARY TAYLOR now MARY MATHES
Recpt. filed for MARY MATHES and LITTLETON MATHES -
their legacy Aug. 13, 1875.

Pg. 6   JOHN RORAX et al. Vs: JNO. MALCOM et al.
$1412.35 ea.
ELIZABETH HUTTON   LUCINDA COOK
POLLY ANN KERR   ELIZA LANE
JANE MALCOM
CAROLINE RORAX
WM. HENRY (minor) J.W. MALCOM is guardian.

Pg. 8   W.M. WILLIAMS & O Vs: W.A. FAIN & O. Nov. 6, 1869. Due
heirs of JOHN B. BRYANT, dec'd., as follows $570.59.
W.A. FAIN and wife, S.A. FAIN
W.M. WILLIAMS and wife, L.C. WILLIAM
GILBERT BLANKENSHIP and wife, E.D. BLANKENSHIP
RAMSEY GRIFFITTS and wife, HESTER GRIFFITTS
AMY E. BRYANT   )
JAMES H. BRYANT   ) minors
MARY BRYANT   )
JOSEPH T. BRYANT)

Pg. 10   JOSEPH LAMON Vs: DAVID LAMON & O. Feb. 3, 1869.
$316.66 ea. Due heirs of DAVID LAMON, dec'd., as fol-
lows:
JOSEPH LAMON   JNO. N. MEANS and wife

2

DAVID LAMON   JAMES LAMON
M. FRENCH & wife   Heirs of MARY A. BROWN, dec'd.

Pg. 12   MCCASLAND Vs: WM. MCCASLAND & O. Aug. 29, 1869.
$237.50 ea. Due heirs of JNO. MCCASLAND, dec'd.
MARY MCCASLAND
WILLIAM MCCASLAND (Sweetwater, Tenn.)
ALEXANDER MCGHEE and wife
JOHN R. LEE and wife (WILLARD, Green Co., Missouri)
GOLDE WILSON and wife
JAMES MCCASLAND (WILLARD, Green Co., Missouri)
JERRY MCCASLAND
SYDIA A. MCCASLAND (WILLARD, Green Co., Missouri)
JOHN H. MCCASLAND
LENORA BLACKBURN (WILLARD, Green Co., Missouri)

Pg. 14   R.H. ANDERSON, & wife, Vs: GILBERT KEENE & O. Feb.
15, 1869. $646.06 ea. Sale of JAMES KEENE lands. Due
heirs as follows:
MALINDA ANDERSON
GILBERT P. KEENE
THURSEY M. KEENE)
M.H. KEENE   ) MALINDA ANDERSON, gdn.
WILLIAM KEENE   )

Pg. 16   W.W. LUSTER et al. Vs: Heirs of HENRY TUCK, Nov. 7,
1868. $232.65 ea. Sale of HENRY TUCK land. Due the
heirs as follows:
W.W. LUSTER and wife
RALPH PEARSON and wife
JACKSON TUCK
J.M. TUCK - gdn. of ROBT L. WEBB
HENRY TUCK - gdn. of HENRY WEBB
EDWARD TUCK
MARY J. TUCK

Pg. 18   WM. WALKER et al. Vs: Heirs of JNO. CAYLOR, dec'd. Feb.
8, 1869. $184.45 ea. Due heirs as follows:
WM. WALKER and wife
ELI CAYLOR
JOSEPH L. WALKER and wife) Represented by

3

BRAXTON CAYLOR   ) WM. HEADRICK
PERRY CAYLOR   ) D.W. EMMETT, gdn.
WM. T. CAYLOR   )

Pg. 20   JAMES HUNT, dec'd. Funds pd. by Clerk R.C. TUCKER to
         Admns. in sale of land. Paid WALKER and LANE ADMS.
         $1831.65. (No heirs listed)

Pg. 22   I.F. BEALS, adm., Vs: G.A. BRIGHT & 0. Jan. 6, 1873.
         $7.67 ea. Estate of SAM B. BRIGHT heirs:
         JULIA A. BRIGHT, Widow   SAM B. BRIGHT
         ARLENA BRIGHT   CHARLES BRIGHT
         HASSIE BRIGHT
         Widow JULIA A. BRIGHT, gdn. of minor children ARLENA,
         HASSIE, SAM B., CHARLY BRIGHT

Pg. 24   J.J. HUDGEONS & M.E. HUMPHREYS Vs: Heirs at Law of
         WM. C. HUMPHREYS, Jul. 21, 1869. Rec'd. from J.H.
         DONALDSON for sale of land $1221.25. $786.68 to credi-
         tors. (No disbursement given)

Pg. 26   MGT. EWING Vs: R. CALDWELL, lunatic. Petition to sell
         land MGT. EWING is the gdn. $293.00.

Pg. 28   JAS. HATCHER and O. Vs: E. HATCHER Heirs $18.15 ea.
         Due as follows:
         JOSEPH HATCHER   RICHARD HATCHER
         WM. HATCHER   NOAH HATCHER
         ALFRED CUNNINGHAM   HETTY HATCHER'S heirs
         JAMES HATCHER   REBECCA FLINN
         E.L. HATCHER   THOMAS HATCHERS' heirs
         J.E. MILLSAPS (ELIZABETH MILLSAPS)
         PRESTON ADAMS
         JAMES E. CATLETT (TROTTER'S Store) Sevier Co.
         REUBEN HATCHER

Pg. 30   Due on 44 Acre tract to each heir is $18.70: On the 60
         acre tract $29.50. Aug. 10, 1875.
         Heirs of JOHN S. GILLESPIE, dec'd.
         W.H. GILLESPIE   JAMES F. GILLESPIE
         C.M. GILLESPIE   W.B.W. HEARTSELL and wife

WM. TOOLE and wife _____ BADGETT and wife
JNO. L. GILLESPIE
The interests of W.H. and C.M. GILLESPIE and WM.
TOOLE & wife held by WM. BELLUE.
(B.F. BADGETT and N.C. BADGETT paid in full)
(WILLIAM TOOLES' heirs - W.P., R.O., and N.E. TOOLE)

Pg. 32   JOHN THOMPSON, dec'd. Petition to sell land Nov. 13,
1871. JOHN D. ALEXANDER, gdn., & O. Vs: JAMES
BLACK & wife et al. $314.00 ea.

E.T. THOMPSON   RACHEL BLACK
WELLS THOMPSON   HILLARDE J. THOMPSON
JOHN THOMPSON   HARRIETT A. WEST
CAMPBELL THOMPSON   MILLARD B. THOMPSON
RACHEL BLACK, dec'd. Husband gdn. of minor heirs.
JOHN D. ALEXANDER, gdn. of E. T. THOMPSON, WELLS
THOMPSON, JOHN THOMPSON. (N.R. WEST and H.A.
WEST signed recpt. for their $100.00)

Pg. 36   JACOB BEST estate. $52.27 dollars in full what is due us
on the sale of dower lands of the JACOB BEST estate. Feb.
14, 1874.
JOHN H. MARTIN (husband)
SALLIE C. MARTIN (wife)

Pg. 38   W.R. BEST et al. Vs: E. BEST et al. $505.71 ea.

W.R. BEST   JAMES M. BEST (assigned to
MARY J. HAMONTREE   R.C. TUCKER)
DOLLY MCCOLLUM   JOHN F. BEST
SARAH C. ARMSTRONG   ELIZABETH C. BEST
(This settlement is wrong there being eight heirs instead of
seven.)

Pg. 40   W.R. BEST et al. Vs: ELIZABETH BEST et al. $441.84 1/4
ea.
W.R. BEST   JAMES M. BEST (R.C. TUCKER)
MARY J. HAMONTREE   ELIZABETH C. BEST
DOLLY A. MCCOLLUM and husband
JOHN F. BEST
SARAH C. ARMSTRONG (WM. A. ARMSTRONG)
DANIEL BEST

5

Pg. 42   Continuation of the above.

Pg. 44   MARY J. COSTNER Vs: JAMES A. HAYS et al. Aug. 7,
         1871 $45.89 2/7ths.
         JAMES A. HAYES loaned to MARY COSTNER
         J. W. HAYES
         MARY COSTNER
         CYNTHIA HAMPTON loaned to MARY COSTNER
         ELIZA STINNETT
         ELIZABETH MCGHEE, dec'd. JAS. MCGHEE, gdn., for his
         own heirs
         BARBARA BRIANT loaned to MARY COSTNER

Pg. 46   H.M. COSTNER & wife Vs: MARTHA T. BEST et al. Dec. 8,
         1873.
         To MARGARET COSTNER and husband $571.30
         TENNESSEE BEST)
         MARTIN L. BEST   ) minor heirs of JACOB BEST, dec'd.
         LAURA BEST   )
         Sale of dower lands in the case of JOHN M. COSTNER, &
         wife, Vs: MARTHA T. BEST
         CALEB BEST $100.00.
         S.C. HINTON for three minor children.

Pg. 48   W.W. LUSTER et al. Vs: Heirs of HENRY TUCK, Dec'd.
  &   "Rec'd of J.A. GREER, Clerk of Bl. Co. Court $207.30
Pg. 49   balance in full of JACKSON TUCKS' interest in the sale of
         HENRY TUCK lands and the sum of $508.20 due EDWARD
         and MARY TUCK out of the sale of HENRY TUCK land.
         Jan. 8 day 1874. W.V. GRIFFITH, gdn. for JACKSON,
         EDWARD & MARY TUCK.

Pg. 50   S.H. GEORGE et al. Vs: BARBARA GEORGE et al. Mar.
         28, 1878.
         Sale of EDWARD GEORGE lands
         S.H. GEORGE $1240.63 4/7ths to each heir.
         R.C. GEORGE
         NOGA ROREX
         JAMES EDWARD GEORGE) MARY J. GEORGE, gdn.
         SAM'L L. GEORGE   )
         KATHLEEN GEORGE

BARBARA C. GEORGE
In the case of HOUSTON GEORGE et al. Vs: BARBARA C.
GEORGE et al. Rec'd of J.A. GREER $420.50 balance of
proceeds of sale of EDWARD GEORGE lands.
W.R. MATLOCK
BARBARA MATLOCK by MADISON COX, atty. in fact.

Pg. 51   SAM ROREX and NOGA ROREX signed for their part.

Pg. 52   Payment to BARBARA C. MATLOCK formerly BARBARA C.
GEORGE and husband W.R. MATLOCK.

Pg. 53   Rec'd of J.A. GREER, county court clerk for Bl. Co.
$204.00 in full of our interest in the home tract of
EDWARD GEORGE, lands purchased by WM. (or Mrs)
GEORGE, Aug. 19, 1874. SAM ROREX and NOGA ROREX.
$26.80 rec'd. J.A. GREER, clerk, part of LUCAS HOOD tract
of the EDWARD GEORGE lands. S.H. GEORGE.

Pg. 54   Continued apportionment of GEORGE lands.

Pg. 55   Rec'd of J.A. GREER, clerk of county ct., $150.00 in part of
what is coming to us out of the sale of EDWARD GEORGE
lands sold by decree of the county court.
KATHLEEN LAWRENCE
J.S. LAWRENCE, Feb. 7, 1877.

Pg. 56   JAMES H. SHAVER et ux Vs: JANE TILLERY et al.
Land sold to W.R. GODDARD for $1,000.00, Oct. 5, 1874,
on 6 and 12 mos. time except 10% paid in hand. 2 notes
executed for $450.00 ea. Sale of the F.W. HAFLEY lands.
Each heir paid $94.70 5/9ths.
HARRIETT HAFLEY   BETTIE A. TILLERY
W.C. HAFLEY (to J.H. SHAVER) CAROLINE HAFLEY
JANE TILLERY   THOMAS HAFLEY
SAMUEL C. HAFLEY   WILLIAM HAFLEY
LUTITIA HAFLEY - J.H. SHAVER, gdn.

Pg. 58   Credit by W.C. HAFLEY. Recpt. dated Feb. 16, 1876, for
$96.75 in full for NANCY C. WEBBS interest in the sale of
the F.W. HAFLEY lands, who was formerly CAROLINE

HAFLEY. She having transferred her interest to W.C. HAFLEY by deed. JANE TILLERY'S interest in sale of HAFLEY land. She gave power of atty. to her husband W.T. TILLERY 19 May 1877.

Pg. 59   Rockford, Tenn. Jan. 1, 1875. For value rec'd. I have transferred to R.I. WILSON, my distributive portion due me for land of my father's estate, F.W. HAFLEY, dec'd., and authorize clerk to pay over to him when due. S.H. HAFLEY rec'd. of R.I. WILSON the transfer of S.H. HAFLEY'S share of his father's, F.W. HAFLEYS, landed estate, Apr. 5, 1875. W.R. GODDARD.
Rec'd. of J.A. GREER, ck., $100.00 from sale of HAFLEY land sold under decree of the county court. I being one of the heirs of said estate and of the age of 21 years this Nov. 2, 1878.
W.W. HAFLEY
HESTER MILLS, Meigs County, Ill.

Pg. 60   JAMES SNIDER et ux Vs: JOHN H. DEARMOND et al. Land sold for $1400.00.
NANCY NUNS   )
JOHN H. DEARMOND   )
MARGARET DEARMOND   ) all rec'd. $205.93 1/3 ea.
MARY H. FROW and husband   )
SUSAN SNIDER   )
CYNTHIA FRENCH   )

Pg. 61 $200.00 Rec'd of J.A. GREER, being part of SUSAN SNIDER'S interest, formerly SUSAN DEARMOND, in sale of JOHN H. DEARMOND'S lands.
$205.93 by THOMAS J. and MARY H. FROW. Recpt. filed.
$205.93 by JOSHUA and CYNTHIA FRENCH. Recpt. filed.
$205.93 by NANCY J. NUNS heirs.
E. NUN gdn. of NANCY J. NUNS heirs.
Rec'd of J.A. GREER, clerk, $6.00 in full of my interest of an heir of JNO. F. DEARMOND, dec'd., in the case of J.L. SNIDER et ux Vs: JNO. H. DEARMOND et al. Oct. 27, 1875.
JAMES L. SNIDER
DAVE E. SNIDER

8

Pg. 62   JAMES M. GREER Vs: JOSEPH C. GREER & DAVID J.
          GREER. Land sold to JOHN ARMSTRONG Oct. 5, 1874, for
          $625.00. $177.19 1/3 each.
          JAMES M. GREER   (estate of my father)
          JOSEPH C. GREER   (name of father omitted)
          DAVID J. GREER

Pg. 64   ALEX KENNEDY et al. Vs: W.P. TOOLE et al. Springs tract
          sold to J.A. DYCHE Aug. 3, 1875, for $500.00. All heirs
          received $57.78.
          WILL GILLESPY (owned by A. KENNEDY)
          CLEMENTINE BADGETTS heirs
          M.E. HEARTSERL (order to A. KENNEDY)
          M.A.H. TOOLE'S heirs (H.I. WILSON, gdn.)
          JAMES F. GILLESPY
          C.M. GILLESPY
          JOHN S. GILLESPY

Pg. 65   W.A.H. TOOLE, dec'd., heirs interest in sale of GILLESPY
          Springs Tract. Rec'd of J.A. GREER, ck., $59.75 in full
          share of the purchase money for GILLESPY Springs Tract
          belonging to minor heirs of JOHN S. GILLESPIE, dec'd.,
          this Feb. 26, 1876. CHAMBERS MCADAMS, gdn.

Pg. 66   Continuation of the above.

Pg. 68   ARCHIBALD FARMER & wife & STEVEN GRAVES Vs:
          JESSE ROGERS et al. Land sold to ARCH FARMER for
          $2600.00 who gave three separate notes Apr. 27, 1875. All
          heirs received same amount $397.20.
          MILLEY J. FARMER
          STEVEN T. GRAVES
          MARTHA ROGERS (transferred to A. FARMER & wife)
          WILLIAM A. GRAVES
          JOHN A. GRAVES) HUGH GAMBLE, gdn.
          MAHALA GRAVES)

Pg. 69   Rec'd of J.A. GREER, clerk, $410.10 in full my share in the
          sale of ADAM GRAVES lands.

9

His
WILLIAM (X) GRAVES
mark
(None of the heirs say who ADAM GRAVES was to them.)

Pg. 70   W.H. TULLOCH et al. Vs: JAMES & MARY A.C. TULLOCH.
Land sold to T.W. COOK for $1200.00, Oct. 29, 1875.
W.H. TULLOCH   Each heir rec'd. $180.95.
GEORGE H. TULLOCH
ELIZA J. HOWARD and husband JOHN R. HOWARD
JAMES C. TULLOCH
MARY A.C. TULLOCH
JOHN M. TULLOCH (conveyed to E.M. TULLOCH)

Pg. 71   WM. H. TULLOCH - recpt. for payment
EVA M. TULLOCH
JAMES C. TULLOCH an heir and being 21 yrs. of age, Mar.
27, 1877.
MARY A.C. TULLOCH now MARY A.C. FIELDS - her regular
gdn., W.B. HOWARD, Sept. 3, 1877.

Pg. 72   A.C. ANDERSON, gdn., Vs: MARGARET L. HAMIL et al.
Land sold to W.H. RAULSTON Sept. 5, 1870, $1,000.00.
Each heir $230.00.
HETTY HAMIL   WM. F. HAMIL
MARY J. HAMIL
MARGARET L. HAMIL

Pg. 73 $65.00 Rec'd of J.A. GREER, clerk, being a part of what
due minor heirs of MARGARET HAMIL, dec'd., as sale of
HAMIL lands. J.P. RAULSTON, gdn. of the minor heirs of
MARGARET HAMIL. MARGARET R. HAMIL lands.

Pg. 74   JOHN N. MCNABB, admr. of JOHN MCNAB, dec'd., Vs:
JAMES N. MCNABB et al. Rec'd over cost of J.H. MCNABB
$204.15. After debts $187.17 left. Sale of JNO. MCNABBS
land. Each heir received $46.79 1/4.
JAMES H. MCNABB
A.T. MCNABB
JOHN MCNABB
J.H. MCCONNELL, gdn. of MARY MCCONNELL, a minor

10

Pg. 75   Rec'd of J.A. GREER $75.00 on the decree in favor of SAMUEL ALEXANDER & MARGARET ALEXANDER formerly MARGARET OAR in the Chancery Court of Bl. Co., Feb 22, 1876. (MCNABB owed ALEXANDERS)

Pg. 76   J.H. MCNABB signature.

Pg. 78   JOHN W. JONES, gdn., Vs: JOHN J. COSTEN et al. Rec'd of J.A. GREER, clerk, $498.81 being in full of JOHN J. JAMES, S. BRICE, MARTHA E. COSTEN, JOHN H. JONES, and HARLIN C. JONES, minors of TRES ANN JONES, formerly TRES ANN COSTENS interest in sale of the BRICE COSTEN lands sold under a decree of county court. I being the regular gdn. of the above mentioned minors this Jan. 19, 1876.
JOHN W. JONES, gdn.

Pg. 80   W.H. GILLESPY et al. Vs: W.P. TOOLE et al. Mountain tract sold to W.W. HEADRICK $150.00 Aug. 3, 1874. Each heir received $13.68 4/7ths.
WILL GILLESPY $13.68 4/7ths JAMES F. GILLESPY
CLEMENTINE BADGETT heirs C.M. GILLESPY
M.E. HEARTSELL   JOHN S. GILLESPY
M.A. TOOLES heirs
Rec'd of J.A. GREER, former clerk of the county court, $13.00 interest of C.M. GILLESPIE in the sale of 100 acres tract of mountain land sold Aug. 29, 1885.
JOHN F. GILLESPIE, atty. for C.M. GILLESPIE.

Pg. 81   Rec'd of J.A. GREER, $14.25 interest of CLEMENTINE BADGETT heirs. B.F. BADGETT, gdn. Apr. 4, 1876. Rec'd of J.A. GREER, $14.25 interest of M.E. HEARTSELL interest in the sale of the tract of land in Millers Cove sold to W.W. HEADRICK. SAM P. ROWAN, atty. & agt. for M.E. HEARTSELL, Oct. 31, 1876. Rec'd of J.A. GREER $13.68 W.H. GILLESPIE Aug. 27, 1877. Rec'd of JAMES A. GREER $13.75 the share of the heirs of JOHN S. GILLESPIE in the proceeds of land sold to W.W. HEADRICK. CHAMBERS MCADONY, gdn., by C.T. CATES. Rec'd of J.A. GREER, clerk, $2.29 the share of the heirs of J.S. GILLESPIE in the interest of J.F. GILLESPIE, dec'd., arising from the sale of

11

lands in this case to W.F. HEADRICK Nov. 7, 1877.
CHAMBERS MCADONY, gdn., by C.T. CATES.

Pg. 82   JOSIAS GAMBLE, gdn., Vs: MOSES GAMBLE et ux et al.
May 2, 1876.
All heirs received $227.77.
ANGELINE F. GAMBLE   JESSE T. IRWIN
LOUISA MCCAMY   LAURA THOMPSON

Pg. 83   Rec'd of J.A. GREER, clerk, $169.00 in part of what is due
W.C. MURPHY as gdn. of LAURA THOMPSON, one of the
heirs of E. NUN, dec'd., which is paid in accordance to
decree of county court rendered at the May term 1876.
This May 3, 1876 power of atty. on file W.C. MURPHY,
gdn., by W.D. MCINLEY in fact for W.C. MURPHY, gdn. of
LAURA THOMPSON. Rec'd of J.A. GREER, clerk, $58.77
balance in full due LAURA THOMPSON, minor heir of LON
THOMPSON, dec'd., in E. NUN estate sale of house and lot
in East Maryville in the case of JOSIAS GAMBLE, gdn., Vs:
MOSES GAMBLE et ux. W.C. MURPHY, gdn. Rec'd. of J.A.
GREER, clerk, $277.77 in full amt. due JESSE T. IRWIN,
minor heir of JAMES IRWIN and MARGARET IRWIN,
dec'd., in E. NUN estate sale of house and lot in E. Maryville. May 2, 1876. JOSIAS GAMBLE, gdn. for JESSE T.
IRWIN. Credit by R.A. and L.F. MCCAMY. Recpt. dated Jul.
2, 1875, filed for the sum of $225.00 being in full their
interest in the E. NUN Estate. ANGELINE GAMBLE recpt.
filed May 6, 1878, for the sum of $92.85.

Pg. 84   ELIZABETH DAVIS et al. Vs: REBECCA GARNER et al. Bill
for partition land sold for $1500.00. Bill cost $125.45 to be
divided among heirs - $1374.55 All received the same
amount.
ELIZABETH DAVIS $229.19 1/6th each
NANCY DAVIS
RACHEL MCCLANAHAN
MARTHA GARNER, dec'd., heirs
JAMES DAVIS. dec'd., heirs
MARGARET S. DAVIS (now dead)
The heirs of MARTHA GARNER, dec'd., are:
REBECCA FARMER $114.54 1/2) MATTHEW GARNER,

ELI GARNER 114.54 1/2   ) gdn.
The heirs of JAMES DAVIS, dec'd., are:
REBECCA GAMBLE   ) $38.18 1/6th to each.
JOHN DAVIS   )
MARGARET DAVIS   )
WM. DAVIS   ) MINERVA DAVIS, gdn.
MARTIN DAVIS   )
ANDREW DAVIS   )
MARGARET S. DAVIS willed her interest to:
ELIZABETH DAVIS $76.36 1/3
NANCY DAVIS
RACHEL MCCLANAHAN

Pg. 85   Rec'd of J.A. GREER, clerk, $230.64 in full amt. due heirs of MARTHA GARNER, dec'd., in the sale of ADAM GRAVES land sold under decree county ct. in the case of ELIZ. DAVIS et al. Vs: REBECCA GARNER et al. I being their regular gdn. This Aug. 1876. MATTHEW GARNER, gdn. of MARTHA GARNER, dec'd., minor heirs.
RACHEL C. MCCLANAHAN & WM. S. MCCLANAHAN recpt. dated Dec. 23, 1876, filed for their interest in full of the JOHN V. DAVIS estate and also being in full their part of the interest of MARGARET S. DAVIS, dec'd., as bequeathed to them under the will in the said JNO. V. DAVIS estate.
ELIZABETH DAVIS (same as above)
MINERVA DAVIS, gdn. of REBECCA GAMBLE, JOHN DAVIS, MARGARET DAVIS, WM. DAVIS, MARTIN DAVIS and ANDREW DAVIS filed her recpt. in full for the interest of said heirs in the sale of lands belonging to the estate of JNO. V. DAVIS, dec'd. Aug. 21, 1876.

Pg. 86
&   Blank.
Pg. 87

Pg. 88   H.S. COSTNER & wife Vs: SARAH J. CARPENTER & ELISHA CARPENTER. Land sold for $776.00 May 20, 1876. Costs $79.89, leaving $691.11.
ADALINE COSTNER and husband $348.05
SARAH J. CARPENTER $348.05

Pg. 89   Rec'd. of J.A. GREER, clerk, $348.05 in full our interest in
          the sale of SAMUEL CARPENTERS lands. Jul. 27, 1876.
          Rec'd. Maryville, Tenn., Jan. 27, 1880, of J.A. GREER,
          clerk, by the hand of J.C.M. BOGLE, deputy clerk, $403.25
          our distributive share in full of the sale of the lands of
          SAMUEL CARPENTER, dec'd.
          J.O. BROWN
          SARAH J. BROWN
          Attest: J.C.M. BOGLE and S.C. HINTON

Pg. 90   JOHN N. MCCONNELL, gdn., Vs: SAMUEL MALCOM et al.
          Land sold Sept. 20, 1875, to SAM'L AIKIN for $600.00 viz.
          $100.00 in hand paid and 3 notes for $166.66 with inter-
          est from date. $69.42 6/7ths each share.

Pg. 91   Rec'd of J.A. GREER, clerk, a part of what is due me on the
          sale of the W.B. MALCOM lands sold by decree of county
          court. Feb. 10, 1877. ($79.00). Rec'd of J.A. GREER, clerk,
          $5.00 in part what due JOHN E. MALCOM and EMMA and
          ALICE MALCOM out of the sale of the W.B. MALCOM
          lands. Signed JOHN N. MCCONNELL, gdn., for JOHN E.
          EMMA and ALICE MALCOM, minor heirs of W.B. MAL-
          COM, dec'd. Rec'd $14.50 from J.A. GREER, clerk, coming
          to me from the proceeds sale of W.B. MALCOM lands by
          decree. PHEBE MALCOM Jan. 14, 1879. Rec'd. from J.A.
          GREER, clerk, $14.50 coming to us from proceeds sale of
          W.B. MALCOM lands, Jan. 14, 1879. G.B. ROSS, N.P.
          ROSS. Nov. 7, 1879 BOGLE paid JNO. N. MCCONNELL,
          gdn., of EMMA MALCOM, ALICE & other minors of W.B.
          MALCOM, dec'd., $25.00 final. Recpt. book P. 108. JOHN
          MCCONNELL. Rec'd Maryville, Tenn. Mar. 1st, 1880, of
          J.C.M. BOGLE D., clerk, $67.71 in full (See final recpt.
          book pg. 127 for G.B. and NANCY ROSS.) If recpt. shows
          less than $60.00 BOGLE to pay diff. to ROSS. If recpt.
          shows more than $60.00 ROSS to pay diff. to buyer.

Pg. 92   J. LAMAR WALLACE & NANCY J. WALLACE Vs: CHARLES
          F. BROADY & W.H. ANDERSON.
          2 tracts of land sold
          1 tract to A.J. HALL for $200.50
          1 tract to J.L. WALLACE for $700.00

Cost $84.00, $816.50 to be divided
NANCY J. WALLACE $408.25
CHARLES F. BROADY $408.25

Pg. 93   Rec'd of J.A. GREER, clerk, $315.50 in full, my interest in
sale of the tract of land of the BROADY estate purchased
by J. LAMAR WALLACE. May 26, 1877.
J. LAMAR WALLACE
NANCY J. WALLACE
Rec'd of J.A. GREER, clerk, $315.50 in full of CHAS. F.
BROADY'S interest in the sale of the tract of land in the
BROADY estate purchased by J. LAMAR WALLACE. Jun.
7, 1877. J. LAMAR WALLACE, gdn., of CHAS. F. BROADY.

Pg. 94   H.M. COSTNER & wife Vs: MARTHA T. BEST et al.:
(Brought forward from pg. 46)

Pg. 95   Rec'd of J.A. GREER, clerk, $260.06 a part due Tenn.,
MARTIN L. and LAURA BEST, minor heirs of JACOB BEST,
dec'd., being in part purchase money in the sale of DOWER
lands of the JACOB BEST estate sold under decree Jul. 21,
1877.
S.C. HINTON, gdn.

Pg. 96   P.H. CLARK & wife Vs: E.C. DEARMOND et al. and R.G.
DEARMOND Vs: E.G. DEARMOND. Land sold for
$1110.00. Bill of cost $167.45 for distribution $932.55 to:
J.H. DEARMOND $133.22 1/7th (all received equal.
shares).
E.C. DEARMOND
MARGARET J. CLARK and husband P.H. CLARK
R.G. DEARMOND
CYNTHIA R. RIMER? (illegible) and husband M.A. RIMER?
(illegible)
JAMES CLARK (P.H. CLARK, gdn.)
M.E. EAGLETON) D.C. EAGLETON, gdn.
G.F. EAGLETON)

Pg. 97   Rec'd of J.A. GREER, clerk, $133.22 in full share of J.H.
DEARMONDS in sale of RICHARD DEARMONDS lands sold

15

by decree Feb. 4, 1878.
W.H. BRAKEBILL.

Pg. 98 P.G. MONTGOMERY et al. Vs: W.H. PORTER et al.
PHOEBE J. PORTER $442.27
HETTIE MONTGOMERY   623.74
MINERVA RUTLEDGE heirs   717.27
JULIET WOODFIN heirs   817.27
SARAH RUSSELL   542.27
P.G. MONTGOMERY   120.70
EVALINE E. PORTER   1417.27
A.C. MONTGOMERY   1345.84
Rec'd. of J.A. GREER $100.00 in part distributive share
due P.G. MONTGOMERY out of the estate of A.C. MONT-
GOMERY, dec'd. Dec. 31, 1878. C.T. CATE, atty. Rec'd. of
J.A. GREER $13.67 in full of the interest of the distributive
share of JNO. S. WOODFIN and COLVILLE M. WOODFIN,
heirs of JULIET WOODFIN, dec'd., in sale of A.C. MONT-
GOMERY lands sold under decree. SAM P. ROWAN, atty in
fact, for J.F. WOODFIN, gdn., R.M. MONTGOMERY. Recpt.
in full filed Feb. 4, 1878, for $128.42. J.C.M. BOGLE, D.
clk.

Pg. 99 Rec'd of J.A. GREER, clerk, $717.27 full interest in estate
of A.C. MONTGOMERY, dec'd., of the minor heirs of
MINERVA LIPSCOMB, dec'd., viz: GEORGE C. RUTLEDGE,
DELIA RUTLEDGE and WM. IRA LIPSCOMB. This sum
includes their distributive share in the sale of the lands. I
being their regular gdn. Mar. 4, 1878. W.D. MCCINLE,
gdn., rec'd. of J.A. GREER, clerk, $134.84 interest in estate
of A.C. MONTGOMERY, dec'd., of the minor A.C. MONT-
GOMERY. I being his regular gdn., Apr. 2, 1878. R.I.
WILSON, gdn., E.E. PORTER recpt. filed in full dated Mar.
5, 1878, for $1417.27. P.J. PORTER recpt. filed in full
dated Feb. 5, 1878, for $442.27. SAMUEL & H.A. MONT-
GOMERY recpt. filed in full Mar. 5, 1878, for $623.74.
SARAH C. RUSSELL recpt. filed in full Mar. 5, 1878, for
$542.27. Rec'd. of J.A. GREER, clerk, $817.27 being in full
of the principle of the distributive share of JOHN S.
WOODFIN and COLVILLE M. WOODFIN, heirs of JULIET
WOODFIN, dec'd., in the sale of A.C. MONTGOMERY lands

16

with a power of atty. duly extended to me by J.F. WOODFIN, gdn. of said heirs. Jun. 25, 1878.

Pg. 100 A.L. PARSONS Vs: J.C. & H.A. PARSONS. Sale of land to S.C. HINTON, gdn. of J.C. and H.A. PARSONS $313.50 Sept. 5, 1876.

A.L. PARSONS	$88.11	pd. Apr. 20, 1878.
J.C. PARSONS	88.11	
H.A. PARSONS	88.11	

Pg. 101 Rec'd of J.A. GREER, clerk, $88.11 in full of A.L. PARSONS distributive share of the proceeds of the sale of J.K. PARSONS lands sold by decree Apr. 20, '78. The same recpt. for the same money is also in the execution docket. R.N. HOOD, atty. in fact.

Pg. 102 JAMES H. MCNABB Vs: JOHN N. MCNABB et al. Land sold for $400.00. Cost $132.25, lef $267.75.

JAS. H. MCNABB	$66.94
A.T. MCNABB	66.94
JOHN N. MCNABB	66.94
MARY A. MCCONNELL, J.H. MCCONNELL, gdn.	66.94

Pg. 103 Rec'd. of J.A. GREER, clerk, $66.94 in full of MARY A. MCCONNELLS distributive share in the sale of the ORR tract of the JNO. MCNABB land. Oct. 8, 1878, J.H. MCCONNELL, gdn.

Pg. 104 J.D. ALEXANDER, gdn., et al. Vs: JAS. A. BLACK et al.: Forward from pg. 34.

Pg. 105 Rec'd. of J.A. GREER, clerk, by the hands of J.C.M. BOGLE D., clerk, $100.00 out of the fund arising from sale of the land in this cause. Jan. 6, 1880. JNO. P. THOMPSON. Rec'd. of J.C.M. BOGLE D., clerk, $214.00 funds arising from sale of lands in this cause and due the heirs of CAMPBELL THOMPSON, dec'd. Jul. 7, 1880, MARTHA A. THOMPSON, gdn., and C.T. CATE, atty.

Pg. 106
&   Pages Blank
Pg. 107

Pg. 108 THOS. J. FROW & wife et al. Vs: JOHN H. DEARMOND et al. Rec'd. of W. GODDARD for Dr. COX.

Pg. 109 Rec'd. Maryville, Tenn., Jan. 7, 1880, of J.A. GREER, clerk, by hands of J.C.M. BOGLE, D., clerk, $22.60 in part of funds realized in the sale of the J.F. DEARMOND lands. JOSH FRENCH. Rec'd. Jan. 24, 1880, of J.A. GREER, clerk, by hand of J.C.M. BOGLE $4.55 part of amount due me as distributive of NANCY NUN, dec'd., in the sale of the lands. MARTHA L. NUN

Remainder of the book is blank.

BLOUNT COUNTY TENNESSEE

CHANCERY COURT

EXECUTION DOCKET BOOK II

February 24, 1872 - February 24, 1893

Copied from the original by:

Albert W. Dockter, Jr.

Pg. 2   MARGARET MCMURRY Vs: The Heirs of WILLIAM
         MCMURRY - Dower - Feb. 24, 1872.

Pg. 3   JOHN W. LACKEY & JOHN L. RUSSELL, admrs., Vs:
         MARGARET MATLOCK & O. - Petition to sell land. Land
         sold Nov. 1, 1869. No distribution given.

Pg. 4   S.C. HINTON, gdn., Vs: SAMUEL LOGAN et al. - Petition to
         sell land. Sold Jun. 13, 1870. No distribution given.

Pg. 5   A.C. ANDERSON, gdn., Vs: MARY J. HAMIL et al. - Petition
         to sell land. Land sold Sept. 5, 1870. Distribution cited in
         JAMES A. GREER Workbook pg. 72.

         JOSIAH HENDERSON et al. Vs: G.W. HENDERSON et al. -
         Petition to sell land. Land sold Mar. 11, 1871.
         Heirs of JOHN HENDERSON, dec'd.
         ELIZABETH JONES
         MARY BROWN
         EDWARD HENDERSON (W.S. GRIFFITTS, gdn.)

Pg. 6   A. & A. MCCLAIN, admrs., Vs: JOHN BLANKENSHIP et al. -
         Petition to sell land. Land sold Mar. 11, 1871. No distri-
         bution given.

         W.D. MCCINLEY Vs: AMI HEADRICK - Petition to sell land.
         Land sold Nov. 6, 1870. No distribution given.

Pg. 7   MARY J. COSTNER Vs: JAMES A. HAYES et al. - Petition to sell land. Land sold Aug. 7, 1871. Distribution: Refer to JAMES A. GREER Workbook pg. 44.

Pg. 8   RILEY MARANVILLE, WILLIAM TRICE, & NANCY J. TRICE - Petition *Ex Parte*. Petition for partition of land. Oct. 30, 1871. Distribution:
W.R. TRICE $15.80. (PRICE ?)

Pg. 9   JOHN D. ALEXANDER, gdn., Vs: JAMES BLACK & wife et al. - Petition to sell land. Sold Nov. 13, 1871. Distribution: Refer to GREER Workbook pgs. 4 & 11.

Pg. 11   JOHN W. JONES, gdn., Vs: JOHN J. COSTEN et al. - Petition to sell land. Failed to sell. Revived Dec. term 1871. Failed to get bid. Distribution: Refer to GREER Workbook pg. 78.

Pg. 12   JAMES MATTHEWS, ex., Vs: LOUISE E. DUNLAP et al. - Petition to sell land. Land sold Apr. 29, 1872. No distribution given.

Pg. 14   WILLIAM RODDY, admr., Vs: JAMES BRIANT et al. - Petition to sell land. Land sold Jun. 3, 1872, for $300.00. No distribution given.

Pg. 15   R.N. HOOD, admr., Vs: JAMES DUNCAN et al. - Petition to sell land. Mar. 4, 1872. No distribution given.

Pg. 16   W.R. BEST & O. Vs: ELIZABETH BEST - Petition to sell land. Land sold during R.C. TUCKERS' admin. Lot #1 to JOHN F. BEST for $1800.00. Lot #4 to H.A. HAMONTREE for $1500.00. Lot #5 to JAMES SWANEY for $150.00. Lot #6 sold to MARY C. NELSON for $326.75. Distribution see GREER Workbook pg. 38-40.

Pg. 17   J.H. ROGERS, admr., Vs: MARTHA ROGERS & O. - Petition to sell land. Sold Dec. 2, 1872, for $127.00. Distribution not given.

Pg. 22   WILLIAM RODDY, admr., of THOMPSON BRIANT, dec'd.

Vs: JAMES BRIANT et al. - Petition to sell lands. No distribution given.

Pg. 23 HOUSTON GEORGE et al. Vs: BARBARA GEORGE et al. - Petition to sell land. Mill tract sold Jul. 7, 1873, for $4750. Tract where RICHARD GEORGE lives, mountain tract, GRESHAN tract, LUCAS HOOD Tract. Distribution: Refer to GREER'S Workbook pg. 50.

Pg. 24 H.M. COSTNER & wife Vs: MARTHA T. BEST et al. - Petition to sell land. Sold Jul. 7, 1873, for $2500.00. Distribution: Refer to GREER Workbook pg. 44 & 94.

Pg. 63 T.R. LEE, admr. of JOHN HACKNEY, dec'd., Vs: DAVID
& HACKNEY, et al. - Land sold to pay debt. Amt. of sales
Pg. 82 $3486.10. Jun. 2, 1879. Distribution:
ELIJAH HACKNEY
AARON HACKNEY
SOPHORONA P. LINDLEY & MILTON LINDLEY, husband.

Pg. 69 E.J. RUSSELL, widow of ISAAC RUSSELL (GRAFFY), dec'd. - *Ex Parte* dower and homestead. Jul. 20, 1880.

Pg. 74 DORCAS MCKENRY, widow, Vs: Heirs of SAMUEL MCKENRY, dec'd. - Dower Mar. 1881.

Pg.77 JOHN H. LOGAN, admr., Vs: HUGH L. LOGAN et al. Dec. 31, 1877 (con't. from pg. 53.). Distribution:

HUGH L. LOGAN	$3.20
MARY J. LOGAN	3.20
MARTHA M. LOGAN	3.20
ALEX. W. LOGAN	3.20
NARCISSA LOGAN	3.20
JOHN H. LOGAN	3.20

Pg. 78 EMILY ROGERS et al. Vs: W.N. DAVIS et al. - (con't. from pg. 64). Distribution:

EMILY ROGERS	$10.75
NANCY M. CUMMINGS	10.75
JOHN S. DAVIS	10.75
LAVINA FARMER	10.75
W.N. DAVIS	10.75

```
PETER H. DAVIS          10.75
G.W. DAVIS (heirs)      10.75
JAMES E. DAVIS          10.75
CALEB F. DAVIS          10.75
SARA C. DUNLAP          10.75
```

Pg. 82   Distribution from pg. 63. (2nd distribution)
        ELIJAH HACKNEY (son) $221.67
        AARON HACKNEY (son)   221.67
        B.F. HACKNEY   221.67
        J.L. HACKNEY   221.67
        ELIZABETH J. BEALS (dau.) 221.67
        DAVID HACKNEY (son)   221.67
        LEVI HACKNEY (son)   221.67
        SOPHRONA P. LINDLEY   221.67
        EDITH MCCLURES' heirs
        To: JAS. F. BEALS, atty. in fact. See power of atty. in file
        Nov. 1, 1880.

Pg. 87   JOHN M. MCCONNELL, gdn., Vs: SAMUEL MALCUM et al.
        Vs: J.A. GREER, clerk, Vs: SAMUEL AIKEN - Refer to
        GREER'S Notebook pg. 90. Distribution:
        SAMUEL MALCUM $75.00 + $7.88
        PHEBE MALCUM   68.35 (balance of her share)
        NANCY J. ROSS   .67 (balance in full)
        JOHN E. MALCUM   82.88
        ALICE MALCUM   82.88 (now SPRINGFIELD)
        EMMA MALCUM   82.88 (now ZACKERY)

Pg. 89   JANE COLTER, widow, Vs: Heirs of R.R. COLTER, dec'd.
        Dower Aug. 20, 1881.

Pg. 105   ANN E. FULTON *Ex Parte* - Years support dis-allowed by
        county ct. Apr. Term 1881. Appealed to supreme ct. -
        Reversed & remanded Sept. Term 1881 of supreme ct.

Pg. 106   MARY CLEMENS Vs: Heirs of - W.C. CLEMENS, dec'd.
        Dower. Apr. 28, 1882.

Pg. 118   W.H. KELLER et ux. Vs: SAMUEL STEPHENS - Con't. from
        pg. 102. Petition to sell land. Sold Jan. 2, 1882, to

SAMUEL STEPHENS for $725.00. Distribution:

SAMUEL STEPHENS	$51.76
DAVID STEPHENS	51.76
TILDA MURR	51.76
R.A. STEPHENS	51.76
RICHARD STEPHENS	51.76
M.N. MURR	51.76
PHEBE J. KELLER	51.76
J.C. STEPHENS	51.76
W.R. STEPHENS	51.76
M.E. KELLER	10.35
GEORGE K. KELLER	10.35
J.L. KELLER	10.35
M.J. KELLER	10.35
L.E. KELLER	10.35
A.R. LONG	25.88
C.J. LONG	25.88
M.E. CLEMENS	25.88
M.J. CLEMENS	25.88

Pg. 117 DORCAS HINTON Vs: Heirs of S.C. HINTON, dec'd. Homestead & dower Feb. Term 1883.

Pg. 119 MARGARET KIDD, dec'd., C.T. CATE, admr. Jan. 6, 1883. Distribution:

MALINDA FRENCH	$3.16
JAMES M. KING	3.16
NANNIE M. HARBIN	3.16
CHARLES J. KIDD	3.16
ADDA KIDD	3.16
EMMA KIDD	3.16

Pg. 120 M.J. MONTGOMERY, widow of W.G. MONTGOMERY, dec'd. Dower & homestead Mar. 3, 1884.

Pg. 121 J.C. MCKENZIE Vs: JERRY HENRY - Partition of house & lot in E. Maryville. Sold Mar. 1, 1884, to J.C. MCKENZIE for $156.00. Distribution:

J.C. MCKENZIE	$25.22
JERRY HENRY	75.88

Pg. 122 E.J. BRIGHT, widow of H.S. BRIGHT, dec'd. *Ex Parte* dower
& homestead.

Pg. 124 JACOB TIPTON, dec'd. Estate - JAMES W. DAVIS, admr. -
Dec. 1, 1884. MANERVA GRAVES, dec'd. (dau. of JACOB
TIPTON) who left as her only heir W. ADAM GRAVES, (a
minor) $33.18. To: PETER H. TIPTON, dec'd., heirs who are
unknown $33.18. Share of SARAH JANE TIPTON in shares
of PETER TIPTON, dec'd. $4.74 she being entitled to 1/7 of
PETER TIPTON'S share. To: DORCAN WOODS, formerly
DORCUS TIPTON, a share of PETER TIPTON, dec'd., share
of PETER TIPTON'S $5.53. To JOHN A. TIPTON a share
5.53. To: J. HARTEN (HORTON?) TIPTON an interest of
PETER TIPTON his dec'd. father in estate of JACOB
TIPTON, dec'd. 5.53.

Pg. 125 JAMES H. MARTIN Vs: W.G. MARTIN, gdn., et al. - Bill to
partition KERR land. Land sold to JAMES H. MARTIN
Jun. 2, 1884, for $575.00. Distribution:

JOHN KERR	$96.21
ELIZABETH KERR	96.21
JAMES KERR	96.21
NANCY KERR	96.21
JAMES H. MARTIN	96.21

Pg. 127 LUCINDA LOGAN, dec'd., PETER BRAKEBILL, admr. -
Settlement made Jul. 24, 1884. Recorded estate record "D"
amount divided among heirs. Distribution:

FLORA E. SINCLAIR (formerly LOGAN)	$10.46
(A.W. SINCLAIR)	
JAMES W. LOGAN	10.46
M.C. CLAYTEN	10.46

Pg. 128 WILLIAM A. LANE et al. Vs: MARY E. LANE et al. - Petition
to sell land. Filed Apr. 8, 1884. 1 tract sold Jul. 7, 1884,
to S.S. HOWARD for $4025.00.

Pg. 133 "FRED BEST" tract Aug. 18, 1884, to W.F. BOLINGER for
1000.00.
"WILLIAM GARNER" tract sold Aug. 18, 1884, to JOHN
LAW for 900.00.

Pg. 151 Distribution:

JOHN R. LANE	$585.09
JAMES L. LANE	585.09
ELIZA J. LANE	585.09
MARTHA A. LANE	585.09
CHARLES M. LANE, minor	585.09
CICERO R. LANE, minor	585.09 (J.C. HOWARD, gdn. of
MAGGIE A. LANE, minor	585.09 minors)
MALINDA E. LANE, minor	585.09

(MAGGIE A. LANE later married W.G. MONTGOMERY & he assumed her guardianship)

W.A. LANE	585.09
M.E. HALL	585.09 (married W.S. HALL)

Pg. 129 W.G. MONTGOMERY et al. Vs: MARGARET A. MONTGOM-ERY et al. - Petition to partition land. Sold Mar. 1, 1884, to W.G. MONTGOMERY for $1130.00.

Pg. 130 Distribution:

	1st Div.	2nd Div.	3rd Div.
G.W. MONTGOMERY (minor)	$36.83	48.95	$54.19
W.G. MONTGOMERY (gdn.)	36.83	48.95	54.19
E.M. MONTGOMERY	36.83	48.95	54.19
MAGGIE A. MONTGOMERY	36.83	48.95	54.19
S.C. MONTGOMERY	36.83	48.95	54.19
E.R. MONTGOMERY (minor)	36.83	48.95	54.19
L.G.? MONTGOMERY	85.78		
JOHN MONTGOMERY	85.78		

Pg. 131 LUCINDA SCOTT b/n/f JOHN P. SCOTT Vs: W.B. SCOTT et al. - Petition to sell house and lot for partition. Land sold Jun. 2, 1884, to LUCINDA SCOTT for $400.00.
The amt. in full set apart to LUCINDA SCOTT as dower out of the estate of her late husband W.B. SCOTT, Sr., Oct. 12, 1885. Signed By: LUCINDA HENRY $42.80.
                                JACOB HENRY

Pg. 133 Distribution:

J.E. BROADY	$86.69
N.F. NUCHOLS	
W.C. BROADY	86.87
MARY J. NUCHOLS	
M.G. WILLIAMS	45.94 (A.T. WILLIAMS)
M.J. MARSHALL	45.69 (L.V. MARSHALL)

```
        ELIJAH NUCHOLS    86.69
        JOHN NUCHOLS      91.39
```

Pg. 140 MARY E. WALKER, widow of SPENCER WALKER, dec 'd. *Ex Parte* homestead & dower. Set apart Nov. 15, 1884.

Pg. 142 VINEY SHAVER, widow of WILLIAM SHAVER, dec'd. *Ex Parte* lay off homestead & dower May 4, 1885.

Pg. 143 M.E. LANE et al., minor heirs of S.D. LANE, dec'd. *Ex Parte* - Homestead set apart 1884.

Pg. 144 MARIAM A. BAYLESS, dec'd. JAMES F. BEALS, admr. - Final settlement and distribution made Jun. 22, 1885. Distribution:

```
        HARRISON BAYLESS    $67.87
        ANDREW V. BAYLESS    67.87
        ALEXANDER BAYLESS    67.87
        SARAH H. BAYLESS     67.87
```

Pg. 145 HETTY A. MONTGOMERY *Ex Parte* widow of SAMUEL MONTGOMERY, dec'd. Dower Mar. 3, 1886.

Pg. 146 THOMAS CARPENTER, dec'd. Estate. SAMUEL F. BELL & T.D. CARPENTER, admrs., w/will annexed. Settlement Sept. 11, 1885. Distribution:

```
        MARY E. SCROGGS     $81.47
        THOMAS B. SCROGGS    81.47
        JOHN M. SCROGGS      81.47
        BRUCE F. SCROGGS     81.47
        HORACE M. SCROGGS    81.47
        JULIA M. SCROGGS     81.47
        BLEUNT L. SCROGGS    81.47
```

Pg. 147 H.L.W. JOHNSON et al. Vs: RICHARD H. JOHNSON et al. - Bill to sell land for partition. Land sold Aug. 10, 1885, to J.T. SAFFELL for $275.00. Distribution:

```
        H.W.L. JOHNSON      $23.13
        E.A. SAFFELL         23.13
        MARIAH JOHNSON       23.13
        S.A. ROSS            23.13
```

```
RICHARD H. JOHNSON    23.13
THOMAS M. JOHNSON     23.13
EVALINE H. RHYNE      23.13
MARGARET FIELDS       23.13
```

Pg. 148 FERDILLA CLEMENS et al. Vs: MATILDA CLEMENS et al. -
Petition to partition. Land partitioned in kind setting apart
1/2 to MATILDA, VINEY, EVE, ELIZA, & HENRY CLEMENS
- the other half ordered sold & sold to L. MCGINLEY Jul. 6,
1885, for $250.00. Distribution:

```
MARY ANN EVERETT  1/5 of amount                    $37.13
H.L. CLEMENS (the share of MARTHA HEADRICK)  37.13
Heirs of JOSEPH CLEMENS, dec'd.                     37.13
Heirs of SALLIE BAKER, dec'd. (six heirs)           37.13
```

Pg. 158 THOMAS BAKER $6.18

```
JAMES BAKER           6.18
SAMUEL BAKER          6.18
ANDERSON BAKER        6.18
SARAH DAVIS           6.18
Heirs of MARY LONG, dec'd. (four heirs)
WILLIAM LONG          1.54
GEORGE LONG           1.54
FRANK LONG            1.54
JAMES LONG            1.54
Heirs of SAMUEL CLEMENS (nine heirs)
FERDILLA CLEMENS      4.12
BETSEY STEPHENS       4.12
LUCRETIA BAKER        4.12
SOLITHY CROP          4.12
MARGARET PLEMONS      4.12
PHEBE CALDWELL        4.12
MARTHA LAW            4.12
DORCAS JAMES          4.12
RACHEL LANE           4.12
```

Pg. 149 MRS. J.M. MCFADDEN, dower and homestead *Ex Parte*.
(Husband not listed).

Pg. 152. MRS. M.E. GAMBLE, widow of JAMES T. GAMBLE, dec'd.
Dower & homestead. Set apart Dec. 1885.

LOUISA WALLACE, widow of CHARLES E. WALLACE, dec'd. Dower & homestead. Set apart Jan. 1886.

Pg. 154 AMANDA BEESON, widow of W.H. BEESON, dec'd. Dower & homestead.

Pg. 157 J.C. HOWARD, admr., of SARAH VAUGHT Vs: WILLIAM VAUGHT et al. - Petition to sell land to pay debts. Land sold to OBADIAH RAY Apr. 5, 1886, for $300.00. Distribution - according to her will goes equally to:

WILLIAM VAUGHT	$2.83
JACKSON VAUGHT	2.83
RICHARD VAUGHT	2.83
SARAH RHAY	1.00
VIRGINIA RHAY	1.00
AMBROSE RHAY	1.00

"Rec'd of BEN CUNNINGHAM, Clerk, $7.34 being the distributive shares of WILLIAM VAUGHT & JACKSON VAUGHT in this cause. Also the 1/5 interest each in the distributive share of RICHARD VAUGHT, who is now dead, whose share goes to MARY R. RING."

"Rec'd of BEN CUNNINGHAM, Clerk $2.00 the amount of the legacy of SARAH RHAY & VIRGINIA RHAY under Will of SARAH VAUGHT, Dec'd. being their distributive shares in this cause."

Pg. 160 P.F. WALKER, admr., of J.J. HUDGEONS, dec'd., Vs: ELIZA HUDGEONS et al. - Land sold to pay debts. 40 A. tract & the revision in homestead and dower sold to MARY ALEXANDER on Mar. 1, 1885, for $540.00.

Pg. 162 PLEASANT HENRY Vs: W.L. HENRY et al. - Land sold for partition. Sold Jun. 7, 1886, to PLEASANT HENRY for $1000.00. Sum of $804.93 equally divided between:

PLEASANT HENRY, Sr.	$176.23
W.L. HENRY	188.73
S.W. HENRY	188.73
PLEASANT HENRY, Jr.	201.23

Pg. 164 W.H. WRIGHT et al. Vs: JOHN CLARK et al. - Petition to sell land for partition. 1300 A. in 3rd & 7th dist. Land

sold Sept. 6, 1886, to W.H. WRIGHT, G.D. KIZER & M.L. RUSSELL, jointly.

W.H. WRIGHT	2/3 undivided interest
G.D. KIZER	1/6 " "
W.L. RUSSELL	" " "

Pg. 165 WILL A. MCTEER, admr., of ANDREW B. MCTEER, dec'd., Vs: NANCY MCTEER et al. - Petition to sell land to pay debts. Land sold Sept. 4, 1886, to Mrs. NANCY
Pg. 166 MCTEER for $1605.00. Ex Parte dower and homestead.

Pg. 167 M.B. WARREN et ux. Vs: FANNIE H. MEAD et al. - Petition to partition land in kind. Filed Oct. 24, 1885. Land partitioned.

Pg. 170 MRS. ANN GILLESPIE Dower & Years Support - Mar. 9, 1887.

Pg. 171 MRS. CLARA WEAGLY Ex Parte homestead 1887.

Pg. 173 SARAH E. HOLLAND Vs: MARY D. HOLLAND - Petition for dower & homestead. Filed Jan. 28, 1887.

Pg. 178 JOHN E. MONTGOMERY et al. Vs: L.L. CALLOWAY et al. - Bill for sale of land for partition. Land sold Sept. 19, 1887, to Mrs. M.E. TIPTON for $1400.00. Distribution:

A.B. MONTGOMERY	$196.95
J.E. MONTGOMERY	196.95
FLORA A. MONTGOMERY,	
S.O. MONTGOMERY, gdn.	196.95
R.G. MONTGOMERY	196.95
E.C. CALLOWAY	196.95 (L.L. CALLOWAY)
S.O. MONTGOMERY	196.95
M.E. TIPTON	196.95

Pg. 180 JANE E. WILCOXEN Vs: ELIJAH SHIELDS et al. - Petition for homestead & dower.

Pg. 181 R.P. MCREYNOLDS Vs: LETITIA ISH et al. - Bill filed to sell land for partition. Land sold May 2, 1887, to R.P. MCREYNOLDS & E.D. JONES jointly for $950. Distribution:

R.P. MCREYNOLDS	2 shares	$430.00
FRANK ISH	1/2 of 1	107.50
LETITIA ISH	1/2 of 1	107.50
DIXIE WELCKER	1/3 of 1	71.66
ALBERT WELCKER	1/3 of 1	71.66
HENRY WELCKER	1/3 of 1	71.66

Pg. 182 DANIEL DUNN et ux. Vs: D.B. LAWSON et al. - Petition to sell land. Sold Dec. 5, 1887, to D.B. LAWSON for $700.25.

Pg. 201 Distribution:

J.D. LAWSON	$73.83
D.B. LAWSON	73.83
MILLIE DUNN	73.83
MARY OLIVER	73.83 (WILLIAM H. OLIVER)
W.H. LAWSON	73.83
J.W. LAWSON	73.83
RHODA HEADRICK	73.83
J.L. LAWSON	73.83
T.J. LAWSON	73.83

Pg. 183 NANCY TAYLOR Vs: ISAAC G. TAYLOR et al. - Petition for homestead & dower. Filed Sept. 26, 1887. Years support.

Pg. 184 NANNIE B. MCCLUNG Vs: JOHN EARNEST MCCLUNG et al. - Petition for homestead & dower. Filed Aug. 3, 1887. Years support.

Pg. 186 M.A. RODDY Nov. 1885 homestead & dower.

Pg. 187 L.W. THOMPSON, admr., Vs: R.A. THOMPSON et al. - Bill filed to sell land to pay debts. Land sold Jun. 7, 1887, to J.E. THOMPSON for $1326.00. Distribution:

L.W. THOMPSON 1/8 share	$98.97
DAVID C. THOMPSON	98.97
ROBERT H. THOMPSON	97.98
JOHN H. THOMPSON	97.98

The heirs of W.H. THOMPSON, dec'd. (four in number)

ROBERT A. THOMPSON	24.49
NAOMI THOMPSON	24.49
W.W. THOMPSON	24.49

ALABAMA GRASTON   24.49
The heirs of MARTHA E. KERR, dec'd. (formerly MARTHA
E. THOMPSON) (ten in number)
JESSE KERR   9.89
WILLIAM KERR   9.89
JAMES B. KERR   9.89
DAVID KERR   9.89
CHARLES KERR   9.89
GIN KERR   9.89
JOHN KERR   9.89
ALABAMA HUTTON   9.89
SARAH HAMONTREE   9.89 (J.C. HAMONTREE)
Heirs of CLABO KERR, dec'd.
DAISY M. KERR   4.94
R.M. KERR   4.94
Pg. 188 Heirs of MARY E. BROWN, dec'd. (six in number)
ANNA LESTER   16.49
KITTIE BROWN   16.49
LAURA BROWN   16.49
SANDY BROWN   16.49
WILLIAM BROWN   16.49
SAMUEL BROWN   16.49
The heirs of NANCY MCCOLLUM, dec'd. (three in number)
KITTIE MONTGOMERY   32.99
MAGGIE MONTGOMERY   32.99
ROBERT MCCOLLUM,   32.99
   (minor, J.B. MCCOLLUM, gdn.)

Pg. 190 J.W. KELLER et al. Vs: J.L. KELLER et al. - Petition to sell
land. Land sold in seven lots:
#1 to W.C. GRINDSTAFF for $100.00 Apr. 18, 1887.
#2 to J.A. KAGLEY for   200.00
#3 to A.B. THOMPSON for   163.75
#4 to JOSEPH W. KELLER   200.00
#5 to G.W. THOMPSON for   54.00
#6 to J.H. KELLER for   80.00
#7 to G.W. KELLER for   130.00
Distribution:
JOSEPH W. KELLAR $57.40
NANCY J. KAGLEY   57.40 (J.A. KAGLEY)
G.W. KELLAR   57.40

31

SUSANNAH GARDNER	57.40 (T.R. GARDNER)
JOHN H. KELLAR	57.40
EVELINDA KAGLEY	57.40 (Z.?A. KAGLEY)
J.T. KELLER	57.40
MARY E. LENG	57.40
SARAH S. THOMPSON	57.40 (A.B. THOMPSON)
SAMUEL KELLER	57.40
PHEBE A. PAYNE	57.40 (S.B. PAYNE)
W.H. KELLAR	57.40
JAMES L. KELLAR	57.40
ROBERT B. KELLAR	57.40

Pg. 191 MARY E. CARVER Vs: CAMPBELL A. CARVER, admr., etc. - Petition for homestead and dower filed 1888.

Pg. 192 JESSE R. JAMES b/n/f et ux. Vs: JAMES F. BEALS, gdn., et al. - Partition of the S.T. BOWERMAN land, dec'd. Jun. 1888.

Pg. 194 J.N. BADGETT Vs: MARTHA E. SIMMONS et al. - Petition to sell land for partition. Land sold to H.J. SNELSEN for $415.00, Aug. 6, 1888.

Pg. 195 Distribution:

MARTHA E. SIMMONS 1/6	$54.48
MARY A. ROGERS	54.48
SARAH STONE	54.48
MILTON RANKIN 1/18	18.16
J.H. RANKIN	18.16
JOHN LARGE	18.16
H.J. SNELSEN 2/6	108.96

Pg. 196 JOHN HATCHER et al. Vs: NOAH HATCHER et al. - Petition to sell land for partition & to sell Bank of Tennessee notes. Land sold Sept. 24, 1888, to NOAH HATCHER for $101.00. Distribution:

POLLY CUNNINGHAM 1/14	$1.35
ELIZABETH MILLSAPS	1.35
The heirs of JANE ADAMS, dec'd.	1.35
ELIJAH L. HATCHER	1.35
REUBAN HATCHER	1.35
DOLLY ANN CATLETT	1.35
JAMES HATCHER	1.35

NOAH HATCHER	1.35
RICHARD HATCHER	1.35
REBECCA EVERETT	1.35
JOSEPH HATCHER	1.35
The heirs of WILLIAM HATCHER, dec'd.	
JESSE HATCHER	.17
ELIJAH HATCHER	.17
MARY ANN JACKSON	.17
JOHN HATCHER	.17
THOMAS HATCHER	.17
ANDERSON HATCHER	.17
REBECCA MAPLES	.17
HETTY REONES	.17
The heirs of HETTY BREWER, dec'd.	
ELIZABETH JACKSON	.27
ELIJAH BREWER	.27
REBECCA ANN STOUT	.27
CATHERINE BAKER	.27
NICHOLAS BREWER	.27
The heirs of THOMAS HATCHER, dec'd.	
N.L. HATCHER	.19
J.E. HATCHER	.19
T.W. HATCHER	.19
R.J. EARLY	.19
M.A. HILL	.19
P.T. DAVIS	.19
M.E. HUGHES	.19

Pg. 197 Distributive shares of bank note funds Mar. 24, 1889.

ELIZABETH MILLSAPS 1/7	6.81
JAMES HATCHER	6.81
REBECCA EVERETT	5.81
J.W. & NOAH HATCHER, jointly	5.10
JOHN HATCHER of WM. 1/8 of 1/2	.85
HETTY REONAS of WM.	.85
The heirs of HETTY BREWER, dec'd.	
ELIZABETH JACKSON	1.36
ELIJAH BREWER	1.36
REBECCA STOUT	1.36
CATHERINE BAKER	1.36
NICHOLAS BREWER	1.36
The heirs of THOMAS HATCHER, dec'd.	

M.L. HATCHER	.97
J.E. HATCHER	.97
T.W. HATCHER	.97
R.J. HATCHER	.97
M.A. HILL	.97
P.T. DAVIS	.97
M.E. HUGHES	.97

Pg. 199 C.D. ROBESON et al. Vs: MARY J. CRYE et al. - Petition for partition. Filed Feb. 7, 1888. Land sold Aug. 6, 1888, to J.B. JENKINS for $386.50.

Pg. 200 Distribution:

MARY J. CRYE	$51.65
MARTHA E. ROBESON	51.65
SARAH M. SCOTT	51.65
C.D. ROBESON	51.65
MARY ROBESON, estate	51.65
FRANK BRIGHT	25.82
IDA BRIGHT	25.82

MARY ROBESON'S estate settled under these proceedings. From sale of land in this cause $51.65. Personal estate from Admr. C.D. ROBESON $37.23 or a total of $88.88. Insolvent estate.

Pg. 203 EDWARD TUCK, dec'd., W.V. GRIFFITTS, admr. - Paid me by W.V. GRIFFITTS, admr. $60.93 the distributive share of NANCY O'NEAL in said estate. Dec. 8, 1888. Pd. NANCY FOWLER $60.93 the share of NANCY O'NEAL. (witness: J.A. FOWLER)

Pg. 204 SUSANNAH TAYLOR et al. Vs: ELIZABETH HICKS et al. - Petition to partition land. Land sold Jan. 5, 1896, to H.O. TAYLOR for $620.00.

Pg. 205 Distribution:

JAMES TAYLOR	$67.20
SARAH KIRBY	67.20
ELIZA WOOLSEY	67.20
MARTHA E. WOOLSEY	67.20
SUSANNAH TAYLOR	67.20
MELISSA CHANDLER	67.20
LUCY CALLAHAN	67.20

The heirs of WILLIAM TAYLOR, dec'd.

GEORGE TAYLOR	9.60
CHARLES TAYLOR	9.60
WILLIAM TAYLOR	9.60
RICHARD TAYLOR	9.60
ELIZABETH HICKS	9.60
MOLLIE TAYLOR	9.60
JO ANNA TAYLOR	9.60

Pg. 207 EVALINE TEFFETELLER Vs: CALVIN TEFFETELLER - Petition for homestead and dower 1888-1889.

Pg. 208 J.H. DONALDSON, admr. of JAMES HOLLAND, dec'd., Vs: SARAH E. HOLLAND et al. - Petititon filed to sell reversion in land to pay debts. Land sold Jan. 5, 1889, to SARAH E. HOLLAND for $300.00.

Pg. 209 J.J. GREER, admr. of EZRA H. LEE, dec'd., Vs: JOHN P. RHEA, gdn., et al. - Petition to sell land to pay debts filed Feb. 7, 1888. Order to sell appealed to the Tennessee Supreme Court.

Pg. 212 SARAH A. MOON Vs: JAMES A. MOON et al. - Dower and homestead. Filed Apr. 10, 1890.

Pg. 216 THOMAS THOMPSON et al. Vs: R.A. STEPHENS et al.- Petition to partition. Filed Nov. 24, 1888. Land sold to THOMAS THOMPSON Apr. 27, 1889, for $275.00.

Pg. 217 Distribution: (Total Amount. - $172.84.) Ten shares at $17.28 as follows:

JAMES THOMPSON	$17.28
JANE THOMPSON	17.28

The heirs of GEORGE THOMPSON, dec'd.

MARGARET THOMPSON	2.88
CAROLINE DOWNEY	2.88
JOHN THOMPSON	2.88
MARTIN THOMPSON	2.88
GEORGE THOMPSON	2.88
TENNIE BOREN	.96
NAOMI BOREN	.96
MARY BOREN	.96

The heirs of WILLIAM THOMPSON, dec'd.

THOMAS THOMPSON	3.45
PEGGY WHITEHEAD	3.45
JOHN THOMPSON	3.45
SUSIE HEATON	3.45
CHARLES RASAR	1.72
LEE RASAR	1.72

The heirs of ANDREW THOMPSON, dec'd.

JOHN H. THOMPSON	1.92
JAMES B. THOMPSON	1.92
WILLIAM THOMPSON	1.92
GEORGE THOMPSON	1.92
ANDREW B. THOMPSON	1.92
JANE MURR	1.92
ELIZABETH KELLER	1.92
NANCY KELLER	1.92
ANDREW KELLER	.64
ISAAC KELLER	.64
PHRONIA KELLER	.64

Heirs of POLLY GARDNER, dec'd.

MATTHEW GARDNER	3.45
JACK GARDNER	3.45
JOHN GARDNER	3.45
BART GARDNER	3.45
MARY GIDEON	3.45

The heirs of JOHN THOMPSON, dec'd.

THOMAS THOMPSON	5.76
JACK THOMPSON	5.76
IBBY CHAPMAN	5.76

The heirs of ROBERT THOMPSON, dec'd.

THOMAS THOMPSON	1.92
JAMES THOMPSON	1.92
SAMUEL THOMPSON	1.92
DAVID THOMPSON	1.92
WILLIAM THOMPSON	1.92
MARY ANN DAVIS	1.92
SARAH E. STEPHENS	1.92
MARGARET J. DAVIS	1.92
WILLIAM FARR	1.92
MARY FARR	.96

The heirs of NANCY GARDNER, dec'd.

THOMAS GARDNER	1.72

JAMES R. GARDNER	1.72
BETSY ANN KAGLEY	1.72
MARGARET KAGLEY	1.72
SLOAN GARDNER	1.72
ANDREW GARDNER	1.72
J. BART GARDNER	1.72
GEORGE GARDNER	1.72
MARTHA WILLOCKS	1.72
LAFAYETTE GARDNER	1.72
The heirs of BETSY KERR, dec'd.	
DAVID KERR	8.64
DOLLY KERR	8.64

Pg. 221 MARY C. JOHNSON Vs: W.H. JOHNSON et al. - Petition for dower and homestead. Filed Aug. 19, 1889.

Pg. 222 W.H. JOHNSON et al. Vs: OLIVER P. JOHNSON - Bill to sell land for partition. Knox County land sold Dec. 13, 1889, to R.C. JOHNSON for $1000.00. Blount County land sold Dec. 14, 1889, to CHAS. E. JOHNSON, Jr., for $344.00. Distribution:

MARY E. COLTER (COKER?)	$429.38
R.C. JOHNSON	429.38
W.H. JOHNSON	429.38
JAMES A. JOHNSON	429.38
M.E. MCCLANAHAN	429.38
E.J. BARNHILL	429.38
CHARLES E. JOHNSON	429.38
O.P. JOHNSON	429.38
JOHN M. JOHNSON	429.38
NINA JOHNSON	429.38

Pg. 225 ALEXANDER B. MCTEER Vs: A.M. TALLENT et al. - Petition to partition filed Sept. 3, 1889. Land sold Nov. 30, 1889, to ALEX. B. MCTEER for $101.00. Value of dower interest $25.79. Distribution:

ALEX. B. MCTEER	$.31
A.M. TALLENT	.31
MARTHA JOHNSON	.31
BETTIE TALLENT	.31
SULA TALLENT	.31

```
JAMES TALLENT              .31
BENJAMIN TALLENT           .31
```

Pg. 226   J.A. CLEMENS et al. Vs: W.E. CLEMENS et al. - Petition to sell land. Filed Oct. 5, 1889. Sold Dec. 14, 1889, to JOHN A. GIBSON for $362.00. Distribution:

```
J.A. CLEMENS         $44.69
DAVID CLEMENS         44.69
MATILDA A. MCCAMY     44.69
W.E. CLEMENS          44.69
JAMES M. CLEMENS      44.69
H.T. CLEMENS          44.69
SAMUEL R. CLEMENS     44.69
```

Pg. 227   R.L. CULTON Vs: SALLY WHEELER et al. - Petition to sell land for partition. Filed Jun. 10, 1889. Sold Oct. 5, 1890, to WILLIAM DUNLAP for $207.00. Distribution:

```
ELIZA COOK           $18.28
SAMANTHA DELOZIER     18.28
ISABELLA TALLY        18.28
MARIAN SPILLMAN       16.28
SALLY WHEELER         18.28
R.C. CULTON           18.28
```
The heirs of FLETCHER SPILLMAN, dec'd.
```
JANE L.O. KELLY        6.09
MARY P. HENSLY         6.09
HARRIET M. LEDFORD     6.09
```

Pg. 228   NANCY MCCOY Vs: ROBERT B. MCCOY et al. - Petition to sell land. Filed Oct. 31, 1889. Sold Feb. 1, 1890, to WILLIAM WILSON for $303.00. Distribution:
```
NANCY MCCOY          $98.81
```
The heirs of GEORGE MCCOY, dec'd.
```
ROBERT B. MCCOY       16.47
DAVID X. MCCOY        16.47
WILLIAM M. MCCOY      16.47
MARGERRY E. MCCOY     16.47
GEORGE MCCOY          16.47
MARY ANN DUNCAN       16.47 (now dead)
```
The heirs of MARY ANN DUNCAN, dec'd.

JENNIE E. MORRISON	4.12
HARRY S. DUNCAN	4.12
HATTIE N. DUNCAN	4.12
MOLLIE M. DUNCAN	4.12

Pg. 230 JOHN H. SHADDAN, admr. et al. Vs: CORA A. MEANS et al. - Petition to sell land to pay debts and for partition. Land sold Aug. 2, 1890, to CHAS. S. MEANS for $900.00.

Pg. 238 Distribution:

CHARLES S. MEANS	$9.71
RUTH B. YEAROUT	9.71
CORA A. MEANS	9.71
MINNIE G. MEANS	9.71
MARY V. MEANS	9.71

Pg. 231 JAMES A. MOORE et al. Vs: JOHN W. MOORE et al. - Petition to sell land to pay debts and for partition. Land sold to J.B. MOORE for $267.00, Mar. 15, 1890.

Pg. 232 Distribution:

JAMES A. MOORE	$28.39
JOSEPH B. MOORE	28.39
MARY R. KEY	28.39
JOHN W. MOORE	28.39
Heirs of LEUIZA J. TALLENT, dec'd.	
C.B. TALLENT	4.05
J.E. TALLENT	4.05
W.A. TALLENT	4.05
MARY J. TALLENT	4.05
D.E. TALLENT	4.05
L.A. TALLENT	4.05
JOHN W. TALLENT	4.05

Pg. 233 JOHN C. TULLOCH et al. Vs: C.B. TULLOCH. Petition to sell land. Filed Jun. 16, 1890. Land sold Sept. 29, 1890, to JOHN C. TULLOCH for $600.00. Distribution:

HETTIE A. FIELDS	$104.16
MARY M. HOYL	104.16 (SAMUEL T. HOYL)
JOHN C. TULLOCH	104.16
C.B. TULLOCH	104.16
M.T. ROSS	34.72
S.M. ARMSTRONG	34.72

W.G. ARMSTRONG   34.72

Pg. 234 W.E. PARHAM et al. Vs: CHARLES L. PARHAM et al. - Petition to sell land. Filed Apr. 22, 1890. Land sold Jun. 16, 1890, to W.T. PARHAM for $2800.00. Distribution:
W.E. PARHAM $400.47
EMMA P. CATES   400.47
ANNA KAISER   400.47
R.A. PARHAM   400.47
CHARLES L. PARHAM   400.47
EDWARD F. PARHAM   400.47
GUY H. PARHAM   400.47

Pg. 235 CLARA L.J. HENRY b/n/f Vs: ROBERT HENRY et al. - Petition to sell land for partition. May 8, 1890. Land sold Aug. 11, 1890, to GEORGE BROWN for $404.00. Distribution:
GEORGE BROWN $172.59
ELLEN BROWN   57.53 (GEORGE BROWN)
CLARA L.J. HENRY   57.53
ROBERT HENRY   57.53

Pg. 236 ANNIE M. WILSON Vs: EDWIN SELLERS et al. - Bill filed Jan. 9, 1891, for partition. House and Lot sold to ANNIE M. WILSON May 16, 1891, for $1950.00. Mountain land sold to J.W. & C.T. CATES for $50.60. Distribution:
ANNIE M. WILSON $1765.96
EDWIN SELLARS   25.97
IRA SELLARS   25.97
MAY SELLARS   25.97
JOPHATA SELLARS   25.97

Pg. 239 J.H. TEDFORD et al. Vs: BAXTER TEDFORD et al. - Bill to sell land for partition. Land sold Jul. 29, 1891, to R.H. TEDFORD for $5250.00. Distribution:
R.H. TEDFORD 5/8 $3116.50
J.H. TEDFORD 1/8   623.30
BAXTER TEDFORD 1/16 311.65
EWELL TEDFORD   311.65
R.A. TEDFORD 1/40   124.66
JOHN H. TEDFORD   124.66

```
OSCAR TEDFORD          124.66
W.D. TEDFORD           124.66
ELIZA TEDFORD          124.66
```

Pg. 240 FOSTER CLARK et al. Vs: R.L. ANDERSEN et al. - Petition
to sell land for partition. Land sold Sept. 9, 1891, to
FOSTER CLARKE for $500.00.

Pg. 241 Distribution:
The heirs of FLORA ANDERSEN, dec'd. (unknown)
The heirs of CATHERINE ANDERSEN, dec'd.

```
MARY E. COCHRAN, dau.                    $8.60
ISAAC H. ANDERSEN, son                    8.60
E.G. ANDERSEN, grandson                   2.87
R.L. ANDERSEN, grandson                   2.87
MYRA ANDERSEN, granddau.                  2.87
```
The heirs of JANE MCCAMPBELL, dec'd.
```
BRUCE MCCAMPBELL, son                     8.60
LEONIDAS MCCAMPBELL, dec'd.               8.60 (sons heir)
HANNAH PECK, dau.                         8.60
```
The heirs of JOHN MCCORMACK MCCAMPBELL, dec'd.
```
JAMES MCCAMPBELL, son                    12.91 (of N.C.)
KATE JENKINS, dau.                       12.91
```
The heirs of MARY B. MITCHELL, dec'd.
```
JAMES M. MCCAMPBELL, grandson             8.60
PRUDENCE CHAMBERS, granddau.              8.60
```
MARY E. HALL, great-granddau., dec'd.
```
H.S. HALL                               1.07) (J.B. HALL,
F.B. HALL                               1.07) gdn. of these
E.W. HALL                               1.07) 4 minors.)
L.M. HALL                               1.07)
GEORGIA MILLER, granddau.               4.30
```
The heirs of BENJAMIN B. MCCAMPBELL, dec'd.
```
JOHN MCCAMPBELL, son                      5.16
JAMES MCCAMPBELL, son                     5.16
SAMUEL S. MCCAMPBELL                      5.16
MARTHA SIMPSON, dau.                      5.16
JAMES MCCAMPBELL, grandson                .86 (the druggist)
WILLIAM MCCAMPBELL, grandson              .86
CHARLES MCCAMPBELL, grandson              .86
MARY BENTLEY, granddau.                   .86
```

MAGGIE NICHOLSON, granddau.   .86
MARTHA SMITH, granddau.   .86
The heirs of JAMES? (JOSEPH?) H. MARTIN, dec'd.
SAMUEL MARTIN, son   10.04
HUGH MARTIN, son   10.04
WILLIAM MARTIN, son   10.04
MARY PARROT, dau.   10.04
JULIA MARTIN, dau.   10.04
FRANCES MARTIN, dau.   10.04
FOSTER CLARKE   146.30
"Rec'd.of BEN CUNNINGHAM, Clerk $25.82 the distributive
shares of MARY E. COCHRAN, ISAAC H. ANDERSON, E.G.
ANDERSON & MYRA ANDERSON in the cause of FOSTER
CLARKE, et al. Vs:" R.L. ANDERSEN. Feb. 27, 1893
(signed).

Pg. 243 JOSEPH LEATHERWOOD et al. Vs: W.L. LEATHERWOOD
et al. - Land partitioned in kind Aug. 1891. Land divided
into eleven shares or lots and each share taxed with 1/11
of the cost or $9.08.

Lot #1	To GEORGE LEATHERWOOD	$9.08
Lot #2	To JOSEPH LEATHERWOOD	9.08
Lot #3	To FRANCES E. THOMAS	9.08
Lot #4	To SARAH LARGE	9.08
Lot #5	To MARY WILSON	9.08
Lot #6	To W.L. LEATHERWOOD	9.08
Lot #7	To THOMAS LEATHERWOOD	9.08
Lot# 8	To JOHN LEATHERWOOD	9.08
Lot #9	To ELIZABETH DENNIS	9.08
Lot #10	To RACHEL WILSON	9.08
Lot #11	To MARTHA ORR	9.08

Pg. 244 JOHN R. BROWN et al. Vs: M.T. BROWN et al. - Petition to
partition Aug. 3, 1891. Land sold Nov. 14, 1891, to J.R. &
E.D. BROWN, jointly, for $800.00. Distribution:
JOHN R. BROWN 2 shares $293.38
ENOCH D. BROWN
The heirs of W.T. BROWN, dec'd.
M.T. BROWN 1/4 of 1   36.67
L.A. BROWN   36.67

CORA M. BROWN   36.67
DEXTER E. BROWN   36.67

Pg. 245 WAYNE L. HAWORTH et ux. Vs: ELBERT RUSSELL et al. - Petition to sell land. Filed Jul. 21, 1891. Land sold Dec. 4, 1891. Town property sold to SARAH A. BEALS for $550.00. Dec. 4, 1891. Mill sold to L(?) or (T?) R. LEE for $235.00 Dec. 4, 1891. Distribution:

EVA HAWORTH $246.56
ELBERT RUSSELL   246.56
RUTH RUSSELL   246.56
(WILLIAM H. BLACK, gdn.)

Pg. 247 THOMAS D. BINGHAM Vs: SAMUEL L. BINGHAM et al. - Petition to sell land for partition and to lay off homestead 1890. Case transferred to the chancery court and costs incident to laying of homestead ordered paid by guardian of minor defendants. J.N. HENRY, gdn. of HANNAH L. BINGHAM, minor.

Pg. 249 J.E. HOWARD, admr. of JOHN R. GARNER, dec'd. Vs: J.A. GARNER, et al. - Petition to partition land to pay debts. 41 1/2 A. sold to J.W. WILLIAMS May 25, 1891, for $550.00. 41 3/4 A. sold to J.A. GARNER for $440.00 May 25, 1891. Distribution:

J.A. GARNER $132.34
HORACE E. WILLIAMSON   132.34
ROSSIE J. MARTIN   44.11) (J.H. MARTIN, gdn. for
MARY E. MARTIN   44.11) these 3 MARTIN chil-
JOHN MARTIN   44.11) dren)

Pg. 251 R.L. HOUSTON et al. Vs: WILLIAM C. FRENCH et al. - Petition to sell land. Filed Apr. 25, 1891. Land sold Jul. 27, 1891, to J.B. FRENCH for $1600.00.

Pg. 257 Distribution:

ISABELLA J. HEADRICK $387.46
M.A. HOUSTON   387.46
MARY C. COULTER   383.94
WILLIAM C. FRENCH   191.97
FLORA P. FRENCH   191.97

(MARY C. COULTER'S share is less because she received her payment in advance of the others.)

Pg. 252 R.P. MCREYNOLDS Vs: IDA JANE MCCULLEY et al. - Petition for sale of house and lot. Filed Jul. 31, 1891. Property sold Oct. 26, 1891, to R.P. MCREYNOLDS for $875.00. Distribution:

ROBERT P. MCREYNOLDS 7 shares	$653.10
IDA J. MCCULLEY 1/6	15.55
ANNA RAULSTON	15.55
MARY M. JONES	15.55
WILLIAM M. MCREYNOLDS	15.55
SARAH T. MCREYNOLDS	15.55
JOHN G. MCREYNOLDS	15.55

Pg. 253 ELIZA J. SPARKS Vs: The heirs at law of N.H. SPARKS, dec'd. Petition for homestead and dower.

Pg. 254 N.C. BOYD et al. Vs: SARAH J. JOHNSON et al. - Petition to sell property. Filed 1892. Main St. house and lot sold Jul. 2, 1892, to C.N. SIMMONS for $1275.00. Cemetery St. house and lot sold to N.C. BOYD for $525.00. Vacant lot on Boyd St. sold to JOHN M. BOYD for $65.00.

Pg. 255 Distribution:

N.C. BOYD	$356.43	
ANN E. KINNAMON	356.43	
SARAH J. BOYD	356.43	
The heirs of W.A. BOYD, dec'd.		
HUGH BOYD	118.81	
ROY BOYD	118.81	
WILLIAM BOYD	118.81	
The heirs of MARY H. HINES, dec'd.		
SARAH J. JOHNSON	44.55	
FLORENCE J. HINES (BURNETT)	44.55	
LEE A. HINES (minor)	44.55)	(JOSEPH F. MC-
STELLA M. HINES (minor)	44.55)	CLURG, gdn.
HARVEY ED. HINES (minor)	44.55)	these 3 minors.)
CORDIA A. HINES	44.55	
JAMES H. HINES	44.55	
NELLIE R. HINES	44.55	

Pg. 256 CORA C. BARTLETT et al. Vs: CARL H. ELMORE et al. - To sell house and lot for partition. Filed Feb. 18, 1892. Property sold to C.N. SIMMONS Apr. 30, 1892, for $705.00. Distribution:

CORA C. BARTLETT	$106.59
ADDISON M. BARTLETT	106.59
ROBERT A. BARTLETT	106.59
CLARA A. BARTLETT	106.59
NELLIE E. CORT	106.59

The heirs of EDITH M. ELMORE, dec'd.
CARL H. ELMORE (minor)   35.53) (EDGAR A. EL-
ROBERT B. ELMORE (minor)   35.53) MORE, gdn. these
FREDERICK A. ELMORE (minor)35.53) 3 minors.)

Pg. 259 THOMAS N. BROWN, admr., Vs: MATILDA H. MCCULLY et al. - Petition to sell land to pay debts. Filed Nov. 27, 1891. Land sold Apr. 16, 1892, to SEBERN LANE for $265.00.

Pg. 260 Distribution:

JANE PARKINS 1/8	13.59
ALVINA HAMPTON	13.59

Pg. 261 MARTHA CRISP, widow of RICE CRISP, dec'd. Homestead set apart Oct. 1892.

MARGARET PARKER, widow of DAVID PARKER, dec'd. Homestead and dower.

Pg. 262 H.P. HOWARD et ux. Vs: LIZZIE GRIFFITTS et al. - Petition for partition and homestead and dower. 1891-2.

Pg. 263 JAMES JEFFERIES et al. Vs: HARVEY J. JEFFERIES et al. - Bill filed to sell land Mar. 7, 1892. Land sold: Blount tract sold Jun. 27, 1892, to JAMES H. JEFFERIES & JOHN E. JEFFERIES for $2090.00. Sevier tract sold to BENJAMIN LANGSTON & HENRY H. OGLE for $250.00.

Pg. 264 Distribution:

H.J. JEFFERIES	$336.74
ISAAC N. JEFFERIES	336.74
CATHERINE C. JEFFERIES	336.74
JAMES H. JEFFERIES	336.74
JOHN E. JEFFERIES	336.74

RUTH J. MCTEER   336.74
WILLIAM M. DAVIS   336.74

Pg. 266   W.H. ALEXANDER et al. Vs: H.S. HALL et ux. - Bill filed to sell land for partition. Filed Nov. 23, 1892. Land sold Feb. 10, 1893, to JACOB FRESHOUR for $475.00. Distribution:

W.H. ALEXANDER 14/24	$218.38
GEORGIA MILLER 4/24	62.40
J.H. MCCAMPBELL 2/24	31.20
H.S. HALL (minor)	15.60) (J.B. HALL,
F.B. HALL (minor)	15.60) gdn. of these
E.W. HALL (minor)	15.60) 4 minor
L.M. HALL (minor)	15.60) HALL children)

Pg. 267   JANE HENRY et al. Vs: RILEY HENRY et al. - Bill to sell land for partition. Filed Feb. 24, 1893. Land sold Jun. 10, 1893, to HANDY & JANE HENRY for $400.00. Distribution:

JANE HENRY 5/16	109.60
HANDY HENRY	109.60
JOHN ALFRED WHITE	109.60
RILEY HENRY 1/16	21.92

End of Book.

BLOUNT COUNTY TENNESSEE COUNTY COURT

EXECUTION DOCKET BOOK II

Apr. 29, 1893 - Feb. 1915

Copied from the original by:

Albert W. Dockter, Jr.

Pg. 1   GEORGE H. SPARKS, Admr., Vs: JAMES A. SPARKS et al.
Sale of land to pay debts. Land sold Apr. 29, 1893, to J.T.
SPARKS. (Contd. on Pg. 6)
Distributive Shares:

GEORGE H. SPARKS	$17.36
DAVID W. SPARKS	17.36
JAMES A. SPARKS	17.36
JOHN T. SPARKS	17.36
EMELINE SPARKS	17.36
MARGARET E. STEPHENSON	17.36
MARTHTA WEAR	17.36
SAMUEL L. SPARKS	17.36
SAMUEL N. SPARKS	17.36
(son of ALFRED SPARKS, dec'd.)	
Children of WILLIAM SPARKS, dec'd.	
ED SPARKS	$4.32
MARGARET LEE SPARKS	4.32
MARTHA EMELINE SPARKS	4.32
WILLIE SPARKS	4.32

Pg. 2   J.A. GRIFFITTS Vs: PHEBE M. GRIFFITTS et al. - Case
Dismissed 1894. Petition for partition. Cost of homestead
to be paid

by PHEBE M. GRIFFITTS	$14.15
1/3 balance to be paid by J.A. GRIFFITTS	10.81
2/3 balance to be paid by J.V. GRIFFITTS	21.62

Pg. 3   LUTICIA BEST, widow of M.C. BEST, dec'd., Vs: R.F. BEST
         homestead & dower 1894.

Pg. 5   G.M.D. MISER, gdn. of heirs of SARAH E. HOLLAND, dec'd.
         Homestead 1894.

Pg. 7   JAMES A. HITCH et al. Vs: MARY L. MORTON et al. 1893.
         SUSAN C. WILLIS $65.60
         MARY J. COWAN   65.60
         J.A. HITCH   65.60
         MARY L. MORTON   10.93
         REBECCA J. MORTON   10.93
         IDA C. MORTON   10.93
         JENNIE H. MORTON   10.93
         JESSE ANN MORTON   10.93
         GEORGE M. MORTON   10.93

Pg. 8   SAMUEL C. DAVIS Vs: GEORGE D. DAVIS. Bill filed for
         partition Jul. 9, 1894.
         Land sold to J.F. DAVIS Sept. 15, 1894.
         SAMUEL C. DAVIS $79.86
         HARRIET M. DAVIS   79.86
         LAURA C. DAVIS   79.86
         MARTHA E. DELOZIER   79.86
         GEORGE D. DAVIS   79.86
         GRACE A. MCCULLOCH   28.42
         JOHN C. MCCULLOCH   28.42
         SAMUEL W. MCCULLOCH   28.42
         SOPHIA CUMMINGS   43.68
         CORA CUMMINGS   43.68
         MAGNOLIA NORTON   42.63
         JOHN NORTON   42.63

Pg. 10   E.G. KEEBLE et al. Vs: R.P. KEEBLE et al. Petition to sell
         land for partition. 2 tracts sold Oct. 6, 1894. Shares dis-
         tributed Oct. 6, 1895.
         E.G. KEEBLE $73.27
         JOHN E. KEEBLE   73.27
         M.C. KEEBLE   73.27
         M.L. KEEBLE   73.27
         M.P. KEEBLE   73.27

M.A. KEEBLE	73.27
S.G. KEEBLE	73.27
R.P. KEEBLE	73.27
BETTIE J. KEEBLE	73.27
M.C. GAMBLE	73.27

Pg. 12
&
Pg. 25

R.P. MCREYNOLDS Vs: PEARL G. WALLACE et al. Petition to sell land in Blount County & A lot in Concord, Tenn. Filed Aug. 17, 1894. Blount County land sold to T.W. QUEENER, Jr. Concord lot to R.P. MCREYNOLDS.

PEARL G. WALLACE	$415.67
R.P. MCREYNOLDS (3 shares)	1247.01
EFFIE HOLLAND	415.67
NORA BELL HOLLAND	415.67
MYRTLE HOLLAND	415.67
SARAH J. HOLLAND	415.67

Pg. 13 MALLIE F. JOHNSON, admx. of AMANDA M. JOHNSON, dec'd. Vs: GEORGE L. JOHNSON. Petition to sell land to pay debts. Filed Mar. 20, 1894. Land sold to B.S. CATTLETT Sept. 29, 1894. After paying all costs there remained $24.85 to be applied to the account of C. PFLANZE for burial case.

Pg. 14 JOHN C. PARSONS et al. Vs: B.I. BINGHAM et al. Petition to sell land. Filed Jul. 7, 1894. Sold 1 tract to VIRGINIA A. BINGHAM & 1 to HENRY LINE.

B.I. BINGHAM	1/7 share	$141.80
W.P. BINGHAM		141.80
MARY E. PARSONS		141.80
G.L. STEWART	1/14	70.90
ANNIE BINGHAM		70.90
WILLIAM BINGHAM		70.90
THOMAS D. BINGHAM	1/35	28.36
SAMUEL L. BINGHAM		28.36
JAMES H. BINGHAM		28.36
HANNAH L. BINGHAM		28.38
VIRGINIA A. BINGHAM		28.36
G.L. MOSIER	1/28	35.45

M.E. MOSIER	35.45
SARAH MOSIER	35.45
MARTHA BINGHAM	35.45

Pg. 16 F.R. BEST et al. Vs: ADELLA YOUNG et al. Bill to partition land. Filed Oct. 25, 1894. JOHN YOUNG paid into the office $151.12 being the amt. charged against the land set apart to ADELLA YOUNG, to be paid to CHARLES BEST to equalize the share of the heirs of M.C. BEST, dec'd. Jan. 15, 1895. (Amounts not given - nor names of heirs)

Pg. 17 B.M. GUDGER, admr. of DORTHULA WHITTEN, dec'd. Next of kin & heirs at law of DORTHULA WHITTEN. Land sold to pay debts Sept. 1894. Purchased by B.M. GUDGER and P.J. HALE. (Contd. on pg.18)

P.J. HALE	$36.07
B.M. GUDGER	23.11
W.O. MCBATH	3.40

Pg. 18 SARAH E. WILLIAMS Vs: C.A. WOODS, admr., et al. Homestead 1895. Bill of cost pd. by SAMUEL WOODS Jun. 4, 1895.

Pg. 19 ED G. KEEBLE Vs: MATILDA C. KEEBLE et al. Land sold for partition Dec. 14, 1894. Homestead tract to E.G. KEEBLE for $2800.00. 15 acre tract to V.B. WALKER. Distribution of home farm:

E.G. KEEBLE	$1302.55
MATILDA C. KEEBLE	260.51
MARTHA A. KEEBLE	260.51
MARION P. KEEBLE	260.51
SINE G. KEEBLE	260.51
MARY L. FARMER	260.51
Distribution of the"Fry Lot"	$38.66:
E.G. KEEBLE	3.86
JOHN E. KEEBLE	3.86
M.E. KEEBLE	3.86
M.L. KEEBLE	3.86
M.P. KEEBLE	3.86
M.A. KEEBLE	3.86
S.G. KEEBLE	3.86

R.P. KEEBLE	3.86
BETTIE J. FARMER	3.86
M.C. GAMBLE	3.86

Pg. 21 MARTHA J. CAMERON Vs: ROY N. ROSE et al. Land sold for partition Feb. 16, 1895, to MARTHA J. CAMERON for $2,000.00.

MARTHA J. CAMERON 3/5	$1112.55
MAMIE B. CAMERON 1/3 of 1/5	123.62
MINNIE B. CAMERON	123.62
ROY R. CAMERON	123.62
ROY N. ROSE 1/4 of 1/5	92.71
HAMMIE L. ROSE	92.71
EDWARD W. ROSE	92.71
SARAH R. ROSE	92.71

Pg. 23 H.J. BURNS Vs: JAMES W. BURNS et al. Land sold for partition Mar. 23, 1895. Sold in 3 tracts: 19 A. to J.W. BURNS, 45 A. to J.H. GILLESPY, 23 A. to M. F. BREWER.

JAMES W. BURNS	$35.56
W.T. BURNS	35.56
H.J. BURNS	71.12
LAWSON BURNS	35.56
M.F. BREWER	35.56
PHEBE A. FANCHER	35.56
ELIZABETH WATERS	35.56
ARTHUR HUSKEY	11.85
ALEXANDER HUSKEY	11.85
LUCY HUSKEY	11.85

Pg. 26 Board of Directors of Maryville College Vs: FLORENCE ANN LEE et al. Paid Jun. 25, 1895, by WILL A. MCTEER, treas. of college, $353.85.

LEWIS LEE 1/7	$38.52
GEORGE LEE, Jr.	38.52
EDWIN LEE	38.52

(C.T. CATE, Sr., gdn. ad. litem & sol. for minor defendants)

Pg. 27 ANDREW ROREX, Jr., et al. Vs: HIRAM ROREX et al. 1895.

| ANDREW ROREX | $62.89 |

FRANK ROREX	62.89
GEORGE ROREX	62.89
HIRAM ROREX	62.89
ABSALOM ROREX	62.89
CHARLOTTE WALLACE	62.89
MOLLIE CARR	62.89
ALICE CARR	62.89
LUELLA ROREX	62.89
FLORENCE MORRIS	62.89
MAGGIE ROREX	62.89

Pg. 30   ELIZABETH HAMILTON Vs: WILLIAM HAMILTON et al.
Petition for homestead. 1895.

Pg. 31   J.M. YEAROUT Vs: I.R. YEAROUT et al. 1895 land sold.

ISABELLA I. YEAROUT	3 shares	$3110.58
JNO. M. YEAROUT	1 share	1036.86
SAMUEL N. YEAROUT	1 "	1036.86

Pg. 32
S.N. YEAROUT	1097.11
J.M. YEAROUT	1333.55
I.R. YEAROUT	3902.66

I.R. YEAROUT'S interest distributed as follows:

FROW & WALLACE, gdns.	59.51
S.N. YEAROUT	708.62
J.M. YEAROUT	784.12
HASSIE HALL	784.12
ALEX HALL	1568.24

(Being shares of S.J. COULTER & N.R. YEAROUT)

Pg. 33   ED SPARKS Vs: JAMES A. SPARKS. Land sold Aug. 1,
1895 140 A.

J.T. SPARKS	5/10	$808.55
N.E. SPARKS	1/10	161.71
MARTHA WEAR		161.71
SAMUEL N. SPARKS		161.71
J.M. STEPHENSEN	1/40	40.43
LIZZIE J. STEPHENSEN		40.43
MARTHA A. STEPHENSEN		40.43
WILLIAM G. STEPHENSEN		40.43
ED SPARKS		40.43
MARGARET L. SPARKS		40.43

MARTHA E. SPARKS 40.43
WILLIE SPARKS 40.43

Pg. 35 JOHN W. MOORE et al. Vs: JAMES A. MOORE et al. Land
sold Sept. 7, 1895.

JOSEPH B. MOORE	2/5ths	$368.16
JOHN W. MOORE	1/5	184.08
CHARLES KEY	1/3 of 1/5	61.36
DAWSON KEY		61.36
DORA KEY		61.36
CORNELIA B. LAMBERT	1/7 of 1/5	26.29
SAMUEL A. TALLENT	1/7 of 1/5	26.29
JAMES TALLENT		26.29
AVERY TALLENT		26.29
DELIA TALLENT		26.29
JEANNETTE TALLENT		26.29
JOHN TALLENT		26.29

Pg. 37 J. WRIGHT CULTON Vs: FRED WILLARD et al. Land sold
Feb. 15, 1896.

J. WRIGHT CULTON	$710.50
FRED WILLARD	355.25
EARNEST WILLARD	355.25

Pg. 39 JAMES MCCAMY et al. Vs: J. HOUSTON SHAVER et al.
& Land sold for partition. Mar. 7, 1896. $617.84.
Pg. 42

JAMES MCCAMY	1/6 of 1/3	$34.32
WILLIAM MCCAMY		34.32
SARAH HOBBS		34.32
MARGARET CARROLL		34.32
MARTHA WOLF		34.32
ELIZABETH MCCAMY		34.32
WILLIAM SHAVER	1/3/of 1/2 of 1/3	34.32
MARY HAYNES		34.32
HETTY PICKENS		34.32
J. HOUSTON SHAVER	1/2 of 1/3	102.97
JOHN SHAVER	1/4/of 1/3	51.48
FREELING SHAVER		51.48
FATE SHAVER		51.48
JESSE SHAVER		51.48

Now deceased heirs: LOU F. FLIPPO, W.E. SHAVER, H.C.

SHAVER, MARY SHAVER, LEWIS SHAVER, and PEARL SHAVER. (The word "PAID" written over each of their names.)

Pg. 40   J.G. MORTON, admr. of S.J. MCCULLOCH, dec'd., VS: HETTY C. MCCULLOCH et al. Insolvent estate land sold to HETTY MCCULLOCH for $40.00, Sept. 7, 1896.

Pg. 41   CATHERINE TAYLOR, widow of JAMES TAYLOR, dec'd., Vs: I.W. TAYLOR et al. Dower and homestead.

R.P. MCREYNOLDS, gdn., Vs: E. DAVIS et al. Homestead 1897.

Pg. 44   JAMES A. WALKER, ex. of W.F. BOLINGER, Vs: NANCY BOLINGER et al. 1896. Land sold to pay debt. No distribution shown.

Pg. 45   ELIZABETH PICKENS, widow of J.P. PICKENS, dec'd. Homestead and dower 1897.

HETTIE BADGETT, widow of AUGUSTINE BADGETT, dec'd. Homestead and dower set apart Mar. 1897.

Pg. 46   B.C. WILLS (WELLS) Vs: HENRY A. WILLS (WELLS?) et al. Petition to sell land.

B.C. WILLS	$55.21
ANNIE E. HOOD	55.21
N.C. HUTTON	55.21
JOHN S. WELLS	55.21
ADIE BEALS	55.21
HENRY A. WELLS	55.21
J.D. WELLS	55.21
CLARA MURPHY	55.21

(Difficult to tell whether the name was WILLS or WELLS.)

Pg. 47   J.A. PICKENS, admr. of JOHN P. PICKENS et al. Land sold May 8, 1897.

Pg. 48   JOHN C. PHELPS Vs. SARAH SALINE PHELPS et al. Petition to sell land. 1897.

JOHN C. PHELPS	$52.15
SARAH SALINE PHELPS	52.15
CLESTIA PHELPS	52.15
ELLA PHELPS	52.15

Pg. 50   O.C. KIDD, widow of L.M. KIDD, Vs: E.F. KIDD et al. Homestead and dower Oct. 14, 1897.

Pg. 51   JOHN C. CATES Vs: W.P. WALLACE et al. Petition to sell land for partition 1897.

W.P. WALLACE	1/2 int.	$160.17
JOHN W. CATES	1/8	40.04
J.C.M. BOGLE		40.04
MARTHA E. CATLETT	1/20	16.02
MATTIE B. CATLETT	1/20	16.02
W.H. CATLETT		16.02
JULIA J. CATLETT		16.02
B.S. CATLETT		16.02

Pg. 52   A.M. RULE, admr. of R.B. MILLER, et al. Vs: D.B. MILLER et al. Apr. 6, 1897. Petition to sell land and pay debts and for partition.

Pg. 53
R.B. MILLER	$542.84
D.B. MILLER	352.40
MARY MILLER	233.26
J.L. MILLER	74.38
T.J. MILLER	74.38
MARSHALL MILLER	18.59
ALBERT MILLER	18.59
J.H. MILLER	4.64
M.L. MILLER	4.64
SARAH J. MILLER	4.64
IDA H. MILLER	4.64
ANNETTA MILLER	4.64
ANDERSON MILLER	4.64
DORTHULA MILLER	4.64
ALBERT MILLER	4.64

Pg. 54   S.H. BADGETT et al. Vs: MARY BADGETT et al. 1897.

Pg. 55
| S.H. BADGETT | $155.62 |
| H.S. BADGETT | 155.62 |

SARAH J. KIDD	159.75
R.P. BADGETT	159.75
J.N. BADGETT	159.75
MARY BADGETT	159.75
GENEVA PICKENS	159.75

Pg. 56   G. NORTON et al. Vs: JOHN A. MCCULLOCH et al. Petition to sell land. Apr. 6, 1897.

Pg. 57

MARTHA E. NORTON	1 share	$114.11
MARY A. HENRY		114.11
ELIZABETH E. BOYD		114.11
LENNIE MCCULLOCH	1/3 of 1	38.04
JOHN D. MCCULLOCH		38.04
HUGH EMMA MCCULLOCH		38.04
GRACE A. MCCULLOCH		38.04
JOHN C. MCCULLOCH		38.04
SAMUEL W. MCCULLOCH		38.04
JOHN A. MCCULLOCH	1/5 of 1	22.52
CORA E. MCCULLOCH		22.52
ANDREW E. MCCULLOCH		22.52
MARTHA W. MCCULLOCH		22.52
ESTELLA A. MCCULLOCH		22.52

Pg. 60   S.R. CUSICK & J.W. DELOZIER, admrs. of JAS. DELOZIER, dec'd., Vs: SAMUEL W. DELOZIER et al. Petition to sell land to pay debts. Jun. 23, 1897.

Pg. 62   W.C. PHIFER et al. Vs: RICHARD PHIFER et al. Land sold for partition & pay debts.

Pg. 63

LEATHA TRUNDLE	$26.57
OPHELIA TRUNDLE	26.57
CLEMMIE TRUNDLE	26.57
ANNA TRUNDLE	26.57
ELLA SCRIBNER	26.57
MARGARET HOBBS	26.57
WILL C. PHIFER	103.54
RICHARD PHIFER	103.54
ROBERT PHIFER	103.54
THOMAS C. JOHNSON	94.69

(The PHIFERS inherited from both the PHIFER and

TRUNDLE Estates - JOHNSON from the PHIFER estate only.)

Pg. 64 ISABELLA J. PEDIGO et al. Vs: JANE ALEXANDER NUCHOLS. Petition for dower 1898.

Pg. 65 J. SHERMAN GREER, admr. of E.J. BEALS, dec'd., Vs: WILLIAM BEALS et al. Petition to sell land to pay debts Nov. 1897.

Pg. 66 S.F. COWAN et al. Vs: J. HOUSTON COWAN et al. Land sold for partition 1898.

SAMUEL F. COWAN	1/6	$192.13
SAMUEL A. COWAN		192.13
THOMAS P. COWAN		192.13
J. HOUSTON COWAN	1/9	128.09
DORA GAMBLE		128.09
MARY GAMBLE	1/9	128.09
NELLIE MCNUTT	1/18	64.04
IRENE MCNUTT		64.04
FRANKIE MCNUTT		64.04

Pg. 68 W.D. WILLIAMS et al. Vs: WILLIAM RODGERS et al. Land sold for partition. 1898.

W.D. WILLIAMS	$47.37
MALVINA GAMBLE	35.53
ALMY HAYS	3.95
LULA N. WILLIAMS	3.95
LILLIAN PASCHAL	3.95
MICHAEL DAMMERON	3.95
WILL RODGERS	3.95
MARY RODGERS	1.97
WILLIE RODGERS	1.97

Pg. 69 J.M. WILLIAMS, Sr., et al. Vs: WILLIAM RODGERS et al. Petition to sell land 1898.

J.M. WILLIAMS, Jr.	$17.68
M.E. ATKINSON	8.84
J.H. WILLIAMS	8.84
WILLIAM RODGERS	2.95
MICHAEL DAMMERON	2.95

ALMA HAYS	2.95
LULA N. WILLIAMS	2.95
MARY RODGERS	1.47
WILLIE RODGERS	1.47
LILLIAN PASCHEL	2.95

Pg. 70 W.P. HOOD Vs: MARGARET E. HOOD et al. Petition to sell land for partition Oct. 1898.

W.P. HOOD	$886.12
MARGARET E. HOOD	40.28
GRACE L. HOOD	40.28

Pg. 71 S.L. JONES, admr., Vs: E.A. JONES et al. Bill filed to sell land for partition to pay debts. Jun. 1897. Insolvent.

Pg. 73 J.T. KELLER Vs: HENRY ROBERT PEDIGO et al. Petition to sell land for partition. J.T. KELLER $620.02. The balance of $155.01 belongs to defendant HENRY ROBERT PEDIGO out of which he is to pay in distribution $47.06 to:

HENRY ROBERT PEDIGO	$11.76
MARY ANNA PEDIGO	11.96
IZORA ELIZABETH PEDIGO	11.76
WILLIAM HOBART PEDIGO	11.76

Pg. 76 W.M. MURRIN et al. Vs: JOHN MURRIN et al. Bill of sale for partition Aug. 1889.

W.M. MURRIN	$94.90
R.E. AMERINE	93.60
NANCY A. ATCHLEY	47.45
MARY A. MURRIN	47.45
JOHN MURRIN	5.27
MARY ANN MURRIN	5.27
CATHERINE MURRIN	5.27
ROBERT MURRIN	5.27
NANCY E. MURRIN	5.27
RACHEL MURRIN	5.27
JOSEPH MURRIN	5.27
WILLIAM MURRIN	5.27
MARIAH MURRIN	5.27

Pg. 77   T.N. BROWN, admr. of MARY PATE, Vs: CATHERINE GUY et al. Mar. 23, 1897. Petition to sell land to pay debts. Sold Jun. 10, 1899. No funds remained after debt payment.

Pg. 78   MELISSA E. CRYE, next friend & C., VS: MARTHA TEDFORD et al. Aug. 3, 1899. Petition for partition in kind.

J.R. CRYE	$42.53
MELISSA CRYE	42.53
M.J. TEDFORD	42.53

Pg. 80   JACKSON DAVIS Vs: GEORGE BROWN et al. Dec. 4, 1899. Petition to sell land for partition....Dismissed Feb. 5, 1900.

Pg. 81   W.B. TAYLOR et al. Vs: R.F. TAYLOR et al. Jan. 23, 1900.
&
Pg. 86

W.B. TAYLOR	$211.87
ELLIS SLEMONS	22.30
JAMES C. TAYLOR	22.30
CATHERINE TURLEY	22.30
LAFAYETTE TAYLOR	9.55
LYCURGUS TAYLOR	9.55
ROBERT TAYLOR	9.55
ELIZABETH J. TAYLOR	9.55
CORNELIA TAYLOR	9.55
DANIEL TAYLOR	9.55
CALVIN TAYLOR	9.55
ELIZ. J. MURDOCK	8.36
JAMES G. TAYLOR	8.36
WILLIAM L. TAYLOR	8.36
RUFUS F. TAYLOR	8.36
JOANNA C. TAYLOR	8.36
SAMUEL R. TAYLOR	8.36
CHARLES M. TAYLOR	8.36
W.G. SMITH	1.67
MARTHA AUSTIN	1.67
MARY MOONEY	1.67
CLYDE SMITH	1.67
ROBERT BROWN	.83
INEZ BROWN	.83
JOHN C. COX	7.96
ELIZA O. COX	7.96
KITTY COX	7.96

HENRIETTA COX	7.96
ELLEN JACKSON	7.96
MAMIE COX SMITH	7.96
NATHANIEL COX	7.96

$66.88 the amount due heirs of REDDEN G. TAYLOR was distributed & paid as shown from ELIZABETH J. MURDOCK to INEZ BROWN. The distributees should have included CHARLES TAYLOR, son of MILTON C. TAYLOR, MAUD AUSTIN TRUSLOVE, dau. of NANCY AUSTIN, nee TAYLOR, and the unknown heirs of PRISCILLA MOORE they each due $6.08. The money was all paid out before this was discovered.

Pg. 82   WILL M. MCTEER et al. Vs: SAMUEL HOUSTON MCTEER et al. May 1, 1900. Bill to sell land for partition.

LORA COULTER	$119.09
JOHN H. MCTEER	119.09
JAMES E. MCTEER	119.09
SAMUEL H. MCTEER	119.09
ANNA C. MCTEER	119.09
WILLIAM L. MCTEER	119.09

Pg. 83   JOHN M. COULTER et al. Vs: ANDREW COULTER et al. Filed Mar. 20, 1900. Bill filed to partition land. Partitioned Jul. 14, 1900.

Pg. 84   WILLIAM J. JOHNSON Vs: MARY J. PITNER - Petition for partition Feb. 19, 1900.

Pg. 87   E.P. FRENCH et al. Vs: C.M. FRENCH et al. Bill to sell land for partition May 28, 1900.

E.P. FRENCH	$102.38
C.M. FRENCH	51.55
J.W. FRENCH	51.03
P.E. FRENCH	51.19
SARAH FRENCH	51.19
LUCY FRENCH	51.19
ANDREW FRENCH	7.36
ELVA FRENCH	7.36
HOMER FRENCH	7.36
WALTER FRENCH	7.36

CHARLES FRENCH	7.36
FLOYD FRENCH	7.36
LILLIE FRENCH	7.36

Pg. 88 W.M. NUCHOLS Vs: HENRY R. PEDIGO et al. In county court. Bill for partition Jan. 26, 1900.

| CORDELIA F. COPELIN | $613.14 |
| LILLIE O. FARARA | 613.14 |

Pg. 90 S.L. DAVIS et al. Vs: SADIE DAVIS et al. - Land sold for partition Aug. 4, 1900.

A.B. DAVIS	$108.61	
JOHN DAVIS	108.61	
WILLIAM DAVIS	108.61	
JAMES R. DAVIS	108.61	
S.L. DAVIS	108.61	
RACHEL HITCH	108.61	(wife of ANDY)
ELLEN HENRY	108.61	(wife of G.R. HENRY)
RACHEL LAW	108.61	
S.R. CUSICK 1/2	54.30	
RACHEL CUSICK	54.30	
WILLIAM DAVIS	54.30	
JOHN DAVIS	54.30	
JAMES R. DAVIS 1/6	18.10	
RACHEL SHERRILL	18.10	
JOHN DAVIS	18.10	
ELLEN DAVIS	18.10	
SADIE DAVIS	18.10	
MINNIE ANDERSON	18.10	

Pg. 91 T.N. BROWN, admr., Vs: BETTY A. CAYLORE et al. - Bill to sell land to pay debts. Jun. 13, 1900.

Pg. 92 R.A. NUCHOLS et al. Vs: WILLIAM E. CLEMENS et al. Petition to sell land for partition Nov. 1, 1900.

R.A. NUCHOLS (SARAH J.)	$246.54
W.E. CLEMENS	9.20
JAMES M. CLEMENS	9.20
H.T. CLEMENS	9.20
SAMUEL R. CLEMENS	9.20
DAVID CLEMENS	9.20

J.A. CLEMENS	8.80
MARTHA E. MCCAMY	2.30
JOHN MCCAMY	2.30
SARAH MCCAMY	2.30
NOLA MCCAMY	2.30

The MCCAMY children were minors of their father JAMES MCCAMY.

Pg. 93   S.L. NUCHOLS Vs: MARGARET WHITEHEAD et al. - Sell
&   land for partition and payment of debts Nov. 19, 1900.

Pg. 104	J.J. WHITEHEAD 1/11	$55.83
&	PORTER WHITEHEAD	55.83
Pg. 112	JOHN WHITEHEAD	55.83
	J. CALVIN WHITEHEAD	55.83
	MARY GRANT	55.83
	CATHERINE CARTER	55.83
	TENNESSEE MEADOWS	55.83
	WILLIAM A. WHITEHEAD	55.83
	S.L. NUCHOLS (SARAH BACON, int.)	55.83
	GEORGE W. WHITEHEAD	55.83
	JERRY CHAMBERLAIN 1/33	18.61
	DAVID CHAMBERLAIN	18.61
	WILLIAM CHAMBERLAIN	18.61

Pg. 95   J.F. DAVIS et al. Vs: ELI GARNER et al. - Bill filed Aug. 27,
&   1900 to sell land for partition. Land sold to HUGH
Pg. 109   GARNER for $1076.00 Nov. 17, 1900.

J.F. DAVIS	$81.11
JAMES C. DAVIS	81.11
JOHN S. DAVIS	81.11
MARY ROGERS	81.11
SARAH DAVIS	81.11
NANCY FINLEY	81.11
MARTHA MCCLANAHAN	79.31
A.J. TAYLOR	243.33
MARGARET MCCLANAHAN	79.31
WILL GARNER	15.86
HUTE GARNER	15.86
EVALINE GARNER	15.86
NANCY GARNER	15.86
ELI GARNER	15.87

Pg. 96   W.B. ROGERS, admr., Vs: A.J. ROGERS et al.- Filed Jan.
 &   3, 1901, to sell land to pay debts and for partition. Land
Pg. 97   sold Mar. 23, 1901 to W.B. ROGER.
          JOHN V. ROGERS $227.35
          M.B. ROGERS   255.98
          L.W. ROGERS   255.98
          W.B. ROGERS   255.98
          A.J. ROGERS   255.98
          M.L. MCCLANAHAN   127.99
          PEARL J. GRAHAM   127.99

Pg. 99   HENRY LINE, admr., Vs: MARGARET WHITEHEAD et al. -
          Filed Sept. 1, 1900. To pay debt and superceded by the
          cause of S.L. NUCHOLS Vs: MARGARET WHITEHEAD et
          al. - (Bill of costs to be paid out of case of S.L. NUCHOLS
          Vs: MARGARET WHITEHEAD.)

Pg. 101   M.B. HACKNEY, admr., et al. Vs: ELIZABETH GREER et al.
          - Filed Sept. 11, 1900. To sell land for partition. Sold Jan.
          7, 1900, to H.L. ROBERTSON.
          J.S. GREER   1/2 $114.34
          MARY JANE SPEARS   1/4   57.17
          ABNER PARKS   57.17

Pg. 103   JAMES S. HENRY et al. Vs: W.M. CARPENTER et al. - Filed
          Jul. 30, 1901 (Date changed). Bill to sell land for partition.
          Sold Sept. 14, 1901, to D.J. COSTNER.
          FLORENCE HUFFSTETLER $108.17
          JAMES HENRY   108.17
          ELLA HENRY   108.17
          EVA HENRY   108.17
          HORACE CARPENTER   108.17 (minor)
          MARY S. HENRY, widow, life estate of $475.00

Pg. 107   J.F. PETERS Vs: N.C. PETERS et al. - Filed Jul. 2, 1901, to
          sell land for partition. Land sold Sept. 12, 1901 to J.F.
          PETERS. Cost of laying off homestead & dower pd. by
          widow, N.C. PETERS.
          J.F. PETERS $115.53
          J.L. PETERS   115.53
          CLIFFORD BROWN)   (minor heirs of HANNAH S.

HERMAN BROWN   )   119.93   BROWN by gdn., B.S.
MYRTLE BROWN   )   BROWN)

Pg. 108 C.R. LOVE Vs: ANDREW HENRY et al. - Filed Feb. 8, 1901,
to sell land for partition. Land sold May 6, 1901, to C.R.
LOVE.
ANDREW HENRY   1/4   15.15

Pg. 110 THOMAS N. BROWN, admr., et al. Vs: T.D. RUSSELL et al.
- Filed May 2, 1901, to pay debts. Land sold to W.P.
BROWN. Amt. for distribution $45.10. (No names given)

Pg. 113 CHARLES EMERT Vs: EDGAR EMERT et al. - Filed Dec.
13, 1901. Sold for partition. Sold Mar. 10, 1902, to G.A.
EMERT.
CHARLES EMERT $33.33
EDGAR S. EMERT   33.33
W.G. EMERT   33.33

Pg. 115 WILLIAM H. SHIELDS Vs: A.J. SHIELDS et al. Filed Apr.
22, 1902. Sold for partition. Sold Aug. 23, 1902, to MARY
J. SHIELDS.
A.J. SHEILDS   1/3 $66.51
OLIE Z. SHIELDS   1/3   66.51
 (heir of ZACHARIAH SHIELDS)
(minor heirs of WILLIAM H. SHIELDS, dec'd.)
JAMES F. SHIELDS   1/6 of 1/18
RACHEL SHIELDS   "
MARY E. SHIELDS   "
ANDREW J. SHIELDS   "
FLORA E. SHIELDS   "
JOHN E. SHIELDS   "

Pg. 116 DANIEL RATLEDGE et al. Vs: MARY MORRISON et al. -
Filed Oct. 5, 1901. To sell land for partition sold Mar. 22,
1902, to ANDREW GAMBLE & E.B. WALLER.
LIZZIE RATLEDGE
GEORGE MORRISON   3/8 To A.K. HARPER$146.26
JAMES MORRISON
ROBERT MORRISON   1/8   48.75
FRED DEPUTY   48.75

ROBERT MORRISON (grandson)		48.75
CHARLES MORRISON		48.75
DAVID DICKERY	1/16	24.39
JOSEPH ROBERTS		24.39

Pg. 117 J.H. SHANE, admr., Vs: FLORA BEESON et al. - Filed Apr. 24, 1902. To sell land to pay debts. Sold Sept. 27, 1902, to FLORA BEESON.

FLORA BEESON	3/5	$213.32
PHEOBE J. SPURGEON	1/5	71.10
LU HENDERSON		71.10

Pg. 118 The following amount was turned into the hands of CLAY CUNNINGHAM, clerk, by G.W. MONTGOMERY, admr. Estate of WILLIAM & MARY BLY, dec'd., being the amount belonging to the 3 minor heirs of BARBARA DUNLAP, dec'd. Oct. 11, 1905.

WILLIAM DUNLAP	$5.58
LENARD DUNLAP	5.58
MARTHA DUNLAP	5.58

Pg. 119 FOSTER CLARKE et al. Vs: Heirs of FLORA ANDERSON, dec'd. Filed May 28, 1902. To sell land for partition sold Oct. 4, 1903, to FOSTER CLARKE, Jr.

Pg. 120 FOSTER CLARKE et al. Vs: Unknown heirs at law of FLORA ANDERSON, dec'd. -

FOSTER CLARKE	482/1000	$560.05
H.M. WILSON	140/1000	171.95
Heirs of SALLIE A.B. (MCCAMPBELL) HALL		
MINNIE F. HALL	1/42	27.66
HELEN HALL		27.66
EVELYN HALL		27.66
MARY E. COCHRAN		27.66
Heirs of FLORA ANDERSON, dec'd., Jan. $82.98		
JAMES MCCAMPBELL	1/28	41.99
Heirs of MARY B. (MCCAMPBELL) MITCHELL		
MARY E. HALL	1/84	13.83
GEORGIA MILLER		"
Ea. heirs of BENJAMIN B. MCCAMPBELL		
SAMUEL MCCAMPBELL	1/420	2.77

JAMES MCCAMPBELL		"
MARTHA SIMPSON		"
JAMES MCCAMPBELL		"
WILLIAM MCCAMPBELL		"
CHARLES MCCAMPBELL		"
MARY BENTLEY		"
MAGGIE NICHOLSON		"
MARTHA SMITH		"
JOHN MCCAMPBELL	1/140	8.30
ROENA STEINER	1/140	8.30
BRUCE MCCAMPBELL	1/56	20.75
Heirs of LEONIDAS MCCAMPBELL		20.75
Heirs of HOUSTON MCCAMPBELL		20.75
J.P. PECK	1/168	6.92
H.L. PECK	"	6.92
JENNIE CLINE	"	6.92

Pg. 121   MEL HUTSELL et al. Vs: LOS HUTSELL et al. Filed Mar. 19, 1903. To sell land for partition sold May 8, 1903, to G.W. HASKELL.

To heirs of MARTHA HUTSELL	$101.97
To heirs of JEFF. HUTSELL	101.97

Pg. 122   MARTHA HUTSELL heirs:

MEL HUTSELL	1/6	17.00
LOU LONG		17.00
LOS HUTSELL		17.00
LEE HUTSELL		17.00
MOLLIE HUTSELL	"	17.00
Minor heirs of ANNIE TEFFETELLER, dec'd.		
ALFORD TEFFETELLER	1/18	5.66
CLARENCE TEFFETELLER	"	5.66
WILLIAM TEFFETELLER	"	5.66

Pg. 123   C.M. KENNEDY et al. Vs: MARY A. KENNEDY et al. - Filed Apr. 30, 1903. Bill to sell land for partition. Sold. Aug. 13, 1903, to MARY A. KENNEDY homestead.

Pg. 124   Cost incident to laying off homestead and dower - Years support to MARTHA CAYLOR, widow of JAMES CAYLOR, dec'd.

Cost incident to setting apart years support and laying off homestead and dower to: SARAH SIMERLY, Sr., dec'd.

Pg. 125 SAMUEL LOGAN, admr. etc., Vs: ELIZABETH LOGAN et al. - Land sold to pay debts, and for partition. Sold Apr. 9, 1904, to Mrs. A.A. BLANKENSHIP.

Life's estate of ELIZABETH LOGAN		$27.20
SAM LOGAN		6.88
CHARLES LOGAN		6.88
JOHN LOGAN	1/4	7.32
J.T. RATLEDGE, natural gdn.		
WRIGHT RATLEDGE	1/8	3.67 minor
WILLIAM RATLEDGE	1/8	3.67 minor

Pg. 127 ELIZABETH A. WEAR Vs: ELIZABETH ANDERSON et al. Filed Jul. 22, 1904. Sell land for partition. Sold Sept. 21, 1904.

ELIZABETH WEAR	1/2	$367.93
ELIZABETH ANDERSON	1/6	122.64
ISABELLA YOUNG	"	122.64
MALCENA ORR	"	122.64

Pg. 128 ANDREW B. THOMPSON Vs: GEORGE THOMPSON et al. - Filed Jun. 16, 1904. To sell land for partition. Sold Sept. 21, 1904, re-opened. Confirmed to ANDREW B. THOMPSON for $136. (To page 136 for distribution of shares.)

Pg. 129 A.C. DAVIS Vs: SUSAN A. JEFFERIES et al. - Filed Apr. 4th, 1904. To sell land for partition. Sold Jul. 27, 1904 to A.C. DAVIS. Bidding re-opened & land sold for $500 to H.M. BROWN.

REBECCA JEFFERIES	minor)	Total of $165.41
WILLIAM ALFRED JEFFERIES	Minor)	for the
BERTHA JEFFERIES	minor)	JEFFERIES thru
JOHN JEFFERIES	minor)	their gdn.,
MAY JEFFERIES	minor)	C.C. HAGGARD
A.C. DAVIS	$198.49	
SUSAN ANN JEFFERIES	33.08	

Pg. 130 THOMAS N. BROWN, admr., Vs: GEORGE LAMON et al. - Filed Feb. 26, 1904. To sell land to pay debts. Sold Sept.

21, 1904, to JOSEPH I. MCILVAINE.

Pg. 131 Cost of setting apart a years support and laying off of homestead to: PEGGY JANE WALLACE, widow of A.H. WALLACE, dec'd.

Cost of setting apart years support and laying off a homestead to: BELLE KITRELL, widow of ROBERT KITTRELL, dec'd.

Cost of setting apart years support and laying off a homestead and dower to: S.E. HUNT, widow of I.T. HUNT, dec'd.

Pg. 132 W.A. LOGAN, admr., Vs: WILLIAM WARD et al. - Filed Jul. 30, 1904, to sell land to pay debts and for partition. Sold Nov. 21, 1904. Bids re-opened and sold. Distribution of shares on pg. 135.

Pg. 134 W.A. CAUGHRON Vs: HENRY COLUMN et al. - Filed Mar. 10, 1905, to sell land for partition. Sold Jul. 21, 1905. Resold Aug. 15, 1905, to W.A. CAUGHRON.

W.A. CAUGHRON		$910.28
MILLIE WRIGHT	1/2 of 1/7 of 1/182	5.99
ARTIE COLUMN		5.99
LOUISE TUCK	1/13	83.82
SAMUEL TUCK	1/26	41.92
SEBE TUCK		41.92

Pg. 135 W.A. LOGAN, admr., Vs: WM. WARD et al. - Distribution of assets from pg. 132.

WILLIAM WARD	1/10	$119.25	
GEORGE WARD		119.25	
R.J. WARD		119.25	
S.C. WARD		119.25	
JAMES WARD		119.25 -	
given to MATTIE FORD, heir of JAS., dec'd.			
SUSANNA STOUT		119.25	
JANE IRWIN		119.25	
JESSE WARD	1/5 of 1/10	23.86)	
NETTIE WARD	"	23.86)	heirs of
NEWTON WARD	"	23.86)	JOHN WARD

```
BESSIE WARD          "        23.86)
SUSIE WARD           "        23.86)
BURGESS WEST    1/4 of 1/10   29.82
SAM WEST             "        29.82
GEORGE WEST          "        29.82
DELLA WEST           "        29.82
Heirs of BURGESS C. WARD a 1/10 $119.24.
```

Pg. 136 ANDREW B. THOMPSON Vs: GEORGE THOMPSON et al. - Contd. from pg. 128.

```
ANDREW B. THOMPSON      2/9         $69.26
GEORGE THOMPSON         1/9          34.63
WILLIAM THOMPSON                     34.63
NANCY KELLAR                         34.63
BETSY KELLAR                         34.63
JANE MURR                            34.63
   (MARY JANE MURR & husband ALEXANDER MURR.)
JOHN ANDREW THOMPSON  15 of 1/9      6.93
CHARLES THOMPSON                     6.93
BENJAMIN THOMPSON                    6.93
FANNIE T. CHAPMAN                    6.93
KATIE THOMPSON                       6.93
ISSAC T. KELLAR       1/3 of 1/9    11.54
A.B. KELLAR                         11.54
SOPHRONIA POTTER                    11.54
```

I, MATTIE THOMPSON, widow of JOHN H. THOMPSON, dec'd., hereby release any and all claims which I may have in this case and agree that his heirs draw the full amount due the heirs of JOHN H. THOMPSON, dec'd.

Pg. 137 G.H. TAYLOR et al. Vs: ANN ELIZA GILLESPY et al. - To sell land to partition. Filed May 6, 1905, sold Aug. 30, 1905, to J.S. MCFADDEN.

Pg. 138 THOMAS N. BROWN, admr., Vs: ADDIE WILLIAMS - Bill filed Sep. 11, 1905, to pay debts. Sold Nov. 18, 1905, W.D. HEADRICK bought 1 lot - JOHN E. RHEA 1 lot total funds. $129.83. Costs $70.43. Amt. pd. T.N. BROWN, admr. $59.40 (Contd. pg. 138 & 139).

Pg. 139 G.H. TAYLOR et al. Vs: ANN ELIZA GILLESPY et al.

HACK GILLESPY	15/36	$603.39
ANN E. GILLESPY	1/12	120.68
NELLIE BROWN	5/96 and 1/8 of 43/672	87.10
G.H. TAYLOR	43/672	92.67
C.G. TAYLOR		92.67
D.R. TAYLOR		92.67
W.A. TAYLOR		92.67
JODA BROWN		92.67
LILLIE GODDARD	1/8 of 43/672	11.58
CARL HICKS		11.58
MINNIE LONG		11.58
JAMES HICKS		11.58
ERNEST HICKS		11.58
GRACE HICKS		11.58
ELIZABETH HICKS		11.58
ERNEST BYERLY	1/2 of 43/672	46.33
FRANK BYERLY		46.33

W.A. LOGAN, admr., Vs: WILLIAM WARD et al. (from pgs. 132 & 135). Order for judgement for re-sale of land Nov. 1905. Re-sold Feb. 2, 1906 to W.A. LOGAN for $2010.00 cash. Amount due WILLIAM WARD $435.96 rec'd. from CLAY CUNNINGHAM, clerk, $119.28 - Amt. due my wards, BURGESS, SAM, GEORGE and DELLA WEST. PAYTON WEST, gdn.

Pg. 142 CYRUS FIELDS et al. Vs: LOSSIE FIELDS et al. Bill filed Oct. 20, 1905. To sell land for partition. Sold Dec. 23, 1905 to W.S.& LULA ALLISON for $805.00.
Distribution:

CYRUS FIELDS	1/4 share	$177.11
LULA ALLISON		177.11
LOSSIE FIELDS		177.11
NONER CANNON, dec'd.		177.11

(NONER died & she willed it to C.H. CANNON)

Pg. 143 MARGARET DRAKE et al. Vs: HOUSTON WATERS et al. - Bill filed Jan. 2, 1905, to sell for partition. Sold Sept. 18, 1905, to W.M. NUCHOLS for $525.00. (I, MARGARET DRAKE, widow of JOHN WATERS, dec'd., hereby waive all my rights title and claim in and to any part of the proceeds of sale of land in this case and ask that all funds in this case be paid to HOUSTON WATERS & JOHNNIE WATERS this Oct. 12, 1906.)

J.H. WATERS $231.59

JOHNNIE WATERS, ward of MARGARET DRAKE, gdn. $231.58.

Pg. 145 ANDREW B. THOMPSON Vs: GEORGE THOMPSON et al. - (from pgs. 128 & 136).

BETSY KELLAR	$34.63
WILLIAM THOMPSON	34.63
KATIE THOMPSON	6.93

(signed also by WILL F. THOMPSON)

Pg. 146 LANGSTON CUTSHAW Vs: LESTER LATHAM et al. - Bill filed to sell land for partition. Jan. 2, 1906. Sold Mar. 19, 1906, to W.J. GRAVES for $951.00. Distribution:

Pg. 147

LANGSTON CUTSHAW	3/9 int.	$297.88
HARVEY A. CUTSHAW	1/9 "	99.30 -

(HARVEY AUDLEY CUTSHAW, minor, L.C. CUTSHAW, gdn.)

MIRA GRAVES	1/9 "	99.30
LESTER LATHAM		99.30
EDD LATHAM		99.30 (EDGAR)
EGG LATHAM		99.30 (EGBERT)
WALTER LATHAM		99.30

Pg. 148 Cost of laying off homestead to: Mrs. R.C. DAVIS, widow of ZEBULON DAVIS, dec'd.

ELIZABETH J. WHITEHEAD Vs: MARTHA J. GREGORY - Cost of years support & homestead.

Mrs. KATIE FRYE Vs: A.B. FRYE et al. - Cost of homestead

Pg. 149 C.P. MCNABB, gdn., Vs: J.T. GAMBLE et al. -

Pg. 150 J.T. GAMBLE Vs: C.P. MCNABB et al. - Cross-files. Bill filed Jan. 27, 1906, cross bill filed Mar. 7, 1906, to sell land for partition. Land sold Jun. 23, 1906. 1 & 2 tracts to J.T. GAMBLE for $7,000.00. 3rd tract to N.J. BROWN for

71

$500.00. Distributive shares:

JAMES T. GAMBLE	1/6 share	$1163.16
MOSES GAMBLE		1163.16
JANE BREWER		1163.16
RACHEL NEWBERT		1163.16
PAUL EDGAR MCNABB	1/7 of 1/6	581.58
CHARLES GAMBLE MCNABB		581.58
PLEASANT HENRY	1/5 of 1/6	232.64
MARY SEATON		232.64
DELLA COULTER		232.64
JOHN BREWER		232.64
JOSEPH BREWER		232.64

Pg. 151 ELIZA DANIEL et al. Vs: ELLEN LAWSON et al. - Bill to sell land for partition. Filed Mar. 24, 1906, sold Jul. 21, 1906, $201.00 (Cont'd. to pg. 167). Distribution:

ELIZA DANIEL, dau.,	1/9 share	$13.62
(signed also by B.B. DANIEL)		
ELLA LAWSON		13.62
(signed also by T.J. LAWSON)		
ANNIE BOWMAN		13.62
(signed also by N.A. BOWMAN)		
MARTHA GODFREY		13.62
(signed also by JOHN GODFREY)		
NANNIE BOWMAN		13.62
(signed also by ALEX BOWMAN)		
FRANCES KIDD		13.62
BESSIE MATLOCK		13.62
MACK MATLOCK		13.62
CONNIE KEY - granddau. - 1/9		13.62

Pg. 153 R.D. FREEDMAN Vs: Mrs. JOHN MATLOCK et al. - Bill filed Aug. 6, 1906. To sell land for partition. Sold Nov. 24, 1906. 71 A. tract sold to J.N. HENRY for $2975.00. House & lot sold to J.T. ANDERSEN for $1200.00 - Re-opened and sold to MARY K. ELLIS for $1,465.00.

Pg. 155 Distribution:

ANNIE B. CALDWELL	1/4 share	$1042.61
ADDIE E. PROFFITT		1042.61
ROBERT P. KIDD		1042.61
BRUCE M. KIDD		1042.61

(minor heir of EDGAR F. KIDD, dec'd., ward of DELLA M. KIDD)

Pg. 156 H.G. LAW et al. Vs: H. LEONARD LAW et al. - Bill filed Aug. 27, 1906, to sell land for partition. Sold Nov. 12, 1906, to H.G. LAW for $2,000.00. Bidding re-opened sold Dec. 3, 1906, for $2450.00 to W.A. LAW, J.T. LAW & LEE PARKER.

Pg. 157 Distribution:

J.L. LAW	1/9 share	$247.42
W.A. LAW		247.42
H.G. LAW		247.42
H. LEONARD LAW		247.42
J.O. LAW		247.42
(JACKSON O. LAW, minor - H.G. LAW gdn.)		
NANCY E. RUSSELL		247.42
(signed also by H.H. RUSSELL)		
MARTHA F. DAVIS		247.42
HARRIS PARKER		247.42
(gdn., LEE PARKER)		
REBECCA LAW	1/5 of 1/9	49.48
WESLEY LAW		49.48
JIMMIE LAW		49.48
ELIZABETH LAW		49.48
ABRAHAM LAW		49.48

Pg. 158 W.G. ARMSTRONG et al. Vs: SAM T. ROSS et al. - Bill to sell land for partition. Filed Dec. 3, 1906, sold Feb. 27, 1907, to HETTIE FIELDS for $2120.00. Distribution:

MARY N. HOYL	$648.10	
S.M. ARMSTRONG	648.10	
HETTY A. FIELDS	648.10	
SAM T. ROSS - minor)		
JOHN ROSS - minor)	$216.03	to their
LANTY M. ROSS - minor)		gdn., G.W. ROSS
W.G. ARMSTRONG	216.03	

Pg. 159 MARY TEDFORD Vs: D.B. GIFFIN. - Bill to sell land for partition. Filed Dec. 1, 1906, sold Feb. 27, 1907, to D.B. GIFFIN for $1,000.00. Distribution:

D.B. GIFFIN	$443.52	
MARY TEDFORD	443.52	

Pg. 160   JOHN E. GAMBLE Vs: S.J. GAMBLE et al. - Bill filed Dec. 31, 1906, to sell land for partition. Sold Mar. 21, 1907. Land re-sold Apr. 6, 1907, to E. HITCH for $1045.00.
Pg. 161   Distribution:

JOHN E. GAMBLE
a 1/5 & a 3/5 of a 1/5 int. or 8/25ths	$276.75
ELIZABETH JANE CAUGHRON a 1/5 int.	$172.96
(E.I. CAUGHRON)	
MARGARET C. GAMBLE	172.96
SAM J. GAMBLE	172.96
SALLIE GAMBLE 1/5 of a 1/5 share	34.59
(SARAH J. GAMBLE)	
LUTIE DUPES	34.59

Pg. 167   ELIZA DANIEL Vs: ELLEN LAWSON - See pg. 151

Pg. 168   GEORGE C. LONG et al. Vs: CHARLEY KAGLEY - Bill filed Feb. 18, 1907, to sell land for partition. Sold Apr. 29, 1907, to J. MCILVAINE for $240.00.
Pg. 169   Re-opened & sale closed May 13, 1907, to JOE MCILVAINE for $299.00. Distribution:

GEORGE C. LONG	1/10 share	$23.28
JACOB T. LONG		23.28
JOHN H. LONG		23.28
W.H. LONG		23.28
JOSEPH LONG		23.28
ALFORD LONG (ALFRED)		23.28
MOLLIE STEPHENS		23.28
SALLY LONG		23.28
SARINA STEPHENS		23.28
IDA KAGLEY	1/5 of 1/10	4.66
FLORENCE KAGLEY		4.66
Father of minors - T.A. KAGLEY		
CHARLEY KAGLEY	minor	4.66
FRANCIS KAGLEY	minor	4.66
LENARD KAGLEY	minor	4.66

Pg. 170 ISABELLA CRISP et al. Vs: JOHN D. HUFFSTETLER et al. - Bill filed Mar. 10, 1907, to sell land for partition. Sold Oct. 5, 1907, to M.A. HUFFSTETLER for $555.00.

Pg. 171 Distribution:

Pg. 172 JOHN D. HUFFSTETLER 1/2 int.		$212.00
& Heirs of SARAH HUTSELL, dec'd.		212.00.
Pg. 181 HESTER MCINTURFF	a 1/7 of 1/2 Int.	$27.29
MOLLIE KIZER		27.29
(S.H. KIZER)		
ISABELLA CRISP		27.29
FRANK HUTSELL		27.29
JOHN D. HUFFSTETLER	1/10 of 1/7 of 1/2	2.73
LISSIE CRYE		2.73
MOLLIE COLLINS		2.73
(M.B. COLLINS)		
LUTITIA BEST		2.73
(J.R. BEST)		
TENNIE LANE		2.73
ANNIE HALE		2.73
(SAMUEL HALE)		
ROBERT HUFFSTETLER		2.73
WILL HUFFSTETLER		2.73
DORA HUFFSTETLER		2.73
CASSIE HUFFSTETLER		2.73
JOE CRISP	1/8 of 1/7 of 1/2	3.41
CHARLIE CRISP		3.41
JOHN CRISP		3.41
WILLIAM M. CRISP		3.41
HENRY CRISP		3.41
SALLIE CRISP (BORUFF)		3.41
(A.H. BORUFF)		
MAHALA CRISP (SWAGGERTY)		3.41
(DELA SWAGGERTY)		
LINN ANN LOWE	14/of 1/7 of 1/2	6.81
DEENY LOWE (DAVIS)		6.81
(DEENY DAVIS - husband G.R. DAVIS)		
EMMA MILLER		6.81
(O.L. MILLER)		
ANNIE KIZER		6.81
OSCAR KIZER		6.81

Pg. 173 ONGUS HENRY et al. Vs: ELSIE BEST et al. - Bill to sell land for partition. Filed Sept 24, 1907, sold Nov. 29, 1907, ONGUS HENRY & DORA HENRY for $1850.00. Distribution:

ONGUS HENRY & DORA HENRY	3/5 share	$1074.18
ELSIE BEST	1/5	358.06
(J.E. YOUNG, gdn.)		
EARL BEST (minor)	1/3 of 1/5	119.35 1/3
GEORGE BEST (minor)		119.35 1/3
(wards of MINNIE BEST, gdn.)		
GERTRUDE BEST (minor)		119.35 1/3

Pg. 174 HOMER NUCHOLS Vs: BEN NUCHOLS et al. - Bill filed Sept. 28, 1907, to sell land for partition. Sold Dec. 12, 1907, for $1850.00. Distribution:

HOMER NUCHOLS	1/3	$617.19
BEN NUCHOLS (minor)		617.19
(ward of W.M. NUCHOLS, gdn.)		
GRACE NUCHOLS (minor)		617.19

Pg. 175 C.G. KEEBLE, admr., Vs: JOHN R. KEEBLE et al. - Bill to sell land to pay debts. Filed Oct. 6, 1906. Land sold Oct. 28, 1907, for $55.00. Bidding re-opened and re-sold Nov. 4, 1907, to W.S. GRAVES for $305.00.

Pg. 176 Distribution:

JOHN R. KEEBLE	1/8 share	$21.75
C.G. REEBLE		21.75
ELIZA JANE GARNER		21.75
(MARSHALL GARNER)		
All minors wards of JOE H. GAMBLE, gdn.		
JAMES E. KEEBLE (minor)		21.75
HUGH L. KEEBLE (minor)		21.75
DOCIE DON REEBLE (minor)		21.75
LUTITIA KEEBLE (minor)		21.75
W. THOMAS REEBLE		21.75
JOHN C. CRAWFORD, power of atty.		

Pg. 177 LOWRY R. KIDD et al. Vs: CHARLEY A. KIDD et al. - Bill filed Jun. 29, 1907, to sell land for partition. Sold Oct. 7, 1907. Farm to J.H. COCHRAN $5,000.00. Vacant Lot to H.G. KIDD for $20.00 Sept. 28, 1907.

Pg. 178 Distribution:

LENA HEADRICK	1/7 share	$661.73
(J.H. HEADRICK)		
CORA MCREYNOLDS		661.73
CHARLES A. KIDD		661.73
LOWRY R. KIDD		661.73
Pg. 179 HORACE G. KIDD		661.73
BLANCHE EDITH KIDD (ALLISON)		661.73
(FRANK ALLISON)		
FERADA LINDSAY KIDD		661.73

Pg. 180 W.M. NUCHOLS, admr., JAS. T. LAW, dec'd., Vs: LIZZIE LAW et al. - Petition filed Feb. 6, 1907, requesting that interest of heirs of J.T. LAW, dec'd., in proceeds of land sale in case of H.G. LAW et al. Vs: H. LEONARD LAW et al. be applied to payment of his debts. Final decree Apr. 25, 1908. Money turned over to W.M. NUCHOLS as admr. of J.T. LAW, dec'd., for payment of bills of dec'd.

Pg. 182 Cost of setting apart years support and laying off homestead to: MARTHA REBECCA GARNER, widow of RANSOM GARNER, dec'd.

Cost of setting apart years support and laying off homestead to: IOWA SCOTT, widow of W.H. SCOTT, dec'd.

Cost of setting apart homestead to: Mrs. WILLIE LAW, widow of J.T. LAW, dec'd.

Pg. 184 SAM W. KEEBLE Vs: ED KEEBLE et al. - Bill to sell land for partition. Sept. 3, 1907. Sold Dec. 30, 1907, to A.S. & N.E. DUNLAP for $400.00.

Pg. 185 Distribution:

SAM W. KEEBLE	1/2 share	$165.79
ED KEEBLE	1/6	55.26
MAUD KEEBLE		55.26 (BRADLEY)
JAMES KEEBLE		55.26

Pg. 186 JOHN B. WELLS Vs: BOYD DAVIS & ELLA MAY WARD. - Bill filed Sept. 3, 1907, to sell land for partition. Sold Dec. 30, 1907, to JOHN B. WELLS for $305.00. Distribution:
JOHN B. WELLS 6/8 share $192.08

BOYD DAVIS   1/8   32.01
ELLA MAY WARD   32.01

Pg. 187 W.A. LOGAN Vs: W.A. HANNAH & JOHN THOMAS - Bill filed May 2, 1908, to sell land to pay debts and for partition. Sold Aug. 15, 1908, to W.J. LEWIS for $2425.00. Distribution:
JOHN THOMAS $738.94. pd. to G.W. MONTGOMERY & wife M.M. MONGOMERY as part of their trust and purchase money for notes held against him in their favor in the land sold in this case.
W.A. HANNAH $648.05 Court decreed this money also to be paid to G.W. MONTGOMERY.

JULIA A. SPARKS et al. Vs: LUCY SPARKS et al. - Bill to sell land for partition and to pay debts. Filed Aug. 1, 1908. Sold Oct. 23, 1908, to H.T. SHULER for $800.00.

Pg. 189 Distribution:
JULIA A. SPARKS	homestead interest	$348.44
JANE SPARKS	1/6 share	23.33
LUCY SPARKS		23.33
BERTIE SPARKS		23.33
JEREME SPARKS		23.33
MAY SPARKS		23.33
JAMES SPARKS		23.33

(SAMUEL N. SPARKS rec'd. $40.00 part payment on his dist. share out of proceeds of land sale.)

Pg. 190 J.T. KINNICK, exec., et al. Vs: NANCY R. ARMSTRONG et al. - Bill filed Aug. 4, 1908, to sell land to pay debts and for partition. Land sold Nov. 23, 1908. 162 A. tract for $5,000.00 & 367 A. tract sold for $100.00 to SAMANTHA LOGAN

Pg. 191 Distribution:
To Foreign Missionary Board Presbyterian Church
                                $2400.47
To estate of J.D. MILLER, dec'd.   2506.67

Pg. 192 J.N. BADGETT Vs: WILLIAM WHITEHEAD et al. - Bill to sell land for partition. Filed Oct. 21, 1908. Sold Jan. 2, 1909, to J.N. BADGETT for $300.00. Distribution:

J.N. BADGETT $119.67
WILLIAM T. WHITEHEAD   minor)
FRANK WHITEHEAD   minor) $119.67
MARY ELLEN WHITEHEAD   minor)
Minors wards of JENNIE WHITEHEAD, gdn.

Pg. 193   GEORGE W. KIRBY et al. Vs: JAMES DRINNEN et al. - Bill
to sell land for partition. Filed Dec. 9, 1908. Sold to J.L.
KIRBY Apr. 5, 1909, for $815.00.

Pg. 194   Distribution:

G.W. KIRBY	1/5 share	$146.70
J.L. KIRBY		146.70
KATIE CARTER		150.55
JAMES DRINNEN	1/3 of 1/5	50.19
ROBERT DRINNEN		50.19
IDA SHARP		50.19
SYLVESTER BREEDEN	1/8 of 1/5	18.82
MARY BREEDEN		18.52
KATIE BREEDEN		18.82
REBECCA BREEDEN		18.82
RUTH BREEDEN		18.82
DIALTHA BREEDEN		18.82
MATTIE DAVIS		18.82
HETTIE MCCALL		18.82

Pg. 195   OLIVER PHELPS et al. Vs: J.S. PHELPS et al. - Bill to sell
land for partition. Filed Jan. 11, 1909. Sold Mar. 25, 1909,
to ROBERT PHELPS for $950.00. Distribution:

J.S. PHELPS		$500.00
OLIVER PHELPS		61.92
ROBERT PHELPS		61.92
WALTER PHELPS		61.92
PEARL PHELPS	(minor)	61.92
INA PHELPS	(minor)	61.92
CHARLIE PHELPS	(minor)	61.92

(J.G. PHELPS, gdn. of minors)

Pg. 196   R.P. MCREYNOLDS Vs: MARY HOPPER et al. - Bill to sell
land for partition. Filed Dec. 30, 1908. Sold May 3, 1908,
to R.P. MCREYNOLDS for $650.00.

Pg. 197   Distribution:

R.P. MCREYNOLDS	5/8 share	$353.53
MARY HOPPER	1/8	70.71
LUCINDA BUNKIS	1/10 of 1/8	7.07
PERRY BOWERMAN		7.07
FRED BOWERMAN		7.07
HATTIE MULTS		7.07
SMITH WINTON		7.07
GEORGIA WINTON		7.07
HELEN WINTON		7.07
GLADDIS WINTON		7.07
LUCY HAMILTON		7.07
LILLIE BEVERLY		7.07
LIZZIE ANDERSON	1/3 of 1/8	23.57
WAYNE BAILEY		23.57
LUCINDA BAILEY		23.57

Pg. 198 A.K. HARPER Vs: HOMER AMERINE - Bill filed May 17, 1909, to sell land for partition. Sold Jul. 27, 1909, to A.K. HARPER for $250.00. Distribution:
HOMER G. AMERINE $67.12
A.K. HARPER 134.23

Pg. 199 Bill of costs and years support homestead and dower for: M.J. GEORGE, widow of S.L. GEORGE, dec'd.

Pg. 200 J.A. MCNUTT and S.T. BROYLES Vs: HENRY C. LAW - Bill to sell land for partition. Filed Sept. 6, 1909. Land sold Dec. 4, 1909, to J.A. MCNUTT & S.T. BROYLES for $2650.00. Distribution:
J.A. MCNUTT $2264.00
S.T. BROYLE
(Rec'd. money together)

Pg. 203 P.W. MILSAPS et al. Vs: CALVIN STAFFORD et al. - Sell land for partition. Filed Sept. 8, 1909. Sold Jan. 29, 1910, to E. GRIBBLE for $120.00.
Distribution:
JASPER MILSAPS 1/5 of 1/3 $5.01
(pd. to EDDIE CLARK, dau. of JASPER, dec'd.)
MARTHA ANN BREWER 5.34
SUSAN ADAMS 5.01

SARAH CLARK (signed with J.W.A. CLARK)	5.01
P.W. MILSAPS	5.01
LUCY ANN STAFFORD	5.01
CALVIN STAFFORD	5.01
ADAM STAFFORD	5.01
JAMES STAFFORD	5.01
MARTHA CARROLL	5.01
MIKE MILSAPS	5.01
MART MILSAPS	5.01
KITTY MILSAPS	5.01
BUD MILSAPS	5.01
NANCY MILSAPS	5.01

Pg. 205 W.B. HOWARD, admr., et al. Vs: JOHN A. WALLACE et al. - Bill to sell land to pay debts and for partition. Filed Mar. 10, 1909. Land sold Oct. 8, 1909 to JOHN A. WALLACE for $2450.00.

Pg. 206 Distribution:

JOHN A. WALLACE	1/7 share	$122.72
LEOTA WALLACE		122.72
LULA LANE	(JOHN LANE)	122.72
BERTIE BUTLER		122.72
ORA WALLACE		122.72
NORA WALLACE		122.72
GEORGIA WALLACE	(minor)	122.72
(SUE WALLACE, gdn.)		

Pg. 207 JAMES R. EVERETT et al. Vs: CHARLES ROMINE. Bill to sell land for partition. Filed May 11, 1909. Sold Sept. 27, 1909, to LUCINDA EVERETT $700.00. Distribution:

FRANK EVERETT	1/6 share	$15.59
JAMES R. EVERETT		15.59
LEM EVERETT		15.59
NANNIE BOYD		15.59
MARGARET J. MCMILLAN	(J.S. MCMILLAN)	15.59
CHARLES ROMINE		15.59

Pg. 208 Mrs. JANE CAMERON et al. Vs: GEORGE M. CAMERON et al. - Bill to sell land for partition. Filed Dec. 23, 1909. Sold Mar. 28, 1910, to JOHN S. BURNS & HENRY MYERS for $3550.00.

Pg. 209 Distribution:
Mrs. JANE CAMERON - value of homestead and dower rts.
$1053.07
NANCY ALICE CAMERON 1/9 - owed note - collected
$131.50

GEORGE CAMERON	1/9	$260.27
CATHERINE SANDS		260.27
BETSY ANN MCCONNELL		260.27
(W.L. MCCONNELL)		
SARAH SUSAN KING		260.27
FRANCIS MARION CAMERON		260.27
WILLIAM ALEXANDER CAMERON		260.27

MARY LOUISE SPARKS 1/9 - owed note collected $48.27
(D.W. SPARKS)
JOHN BROOKS CAMERON 1/9 $160.27 after deducting ct.
order of $100.00

Pg. 210 J.T. KINNICK, admr. of S.B. MCTEER, dec'd., et al. Vs: IDA
KIZER et al. - Bill filed Jun. 12, 1909, to sell land for parti-
tion and pay debts. Land sold Feb. 7, 1910, to HARRIET
C.J. HENRY for $425.50. Distribution:

H.C.J. HENRY	$101.04
J.T. KINNICK	101.04
DEAN heirs (as follows)	101.04
WALTER E. DEAN	16.84
GEORGE A. DEAN	16.84
THOMAS DEAN	16.84
NELLIE DEAN	16.84
JESSIE DEAN	16.84
HARRY O. DEAN	16.84

Pg. 211 SHERMAN SCOTT Vs: ANDREW SCOTT et al. - Petition to
partition land. Filed Jun. 22, 1910. Decree confirming
petition Aug. 13, 1910.

Pg. 212 P.E. HEADRICK et al. Vs: CHARLES L. HEADRICK et al. -
Bill to sell land for partition. Filed Mar. 23, 1910. Sold
Jun. 17, 1910, to SARAH COX for $965.00. 1st. Tract bid
by J.R. DAVIS for $1561.00. 2nd Tract SARAH COX for
$369.00.

Pg. 213	Distribution:	1st.Distr.	2nd.Distr.	3rd.Distr.
1/14	P.E. HEADRICK	$77.73	$56.65	$44.45
	SALLIE COX	77.73	56.65	44.45
	MARTHA J. MURPHY	77.73	56.65	44.45
	ORZELLA CALDWELL	77.73	56.65	44.45
	CHARLES L. HEADRICK	77.73	56.65	44.45
	JAMES H. HEADRICK	77.73	56.65	44.45
	JOHN H. HEADRICK	77.73	56.65	44.45
Pg. 214	WILLIAM W. HEADRICK	77.73	56.65	44.45
	NANCY COWAN	77.73	56.65	44.45
	ANNIE HARMON	77.73	56.65	44.45
	ANNIE MCGINLEY	77.73	56.65	44.45
1/84	LORA COULTER	12.95	9.44	7.40
	JOHN MCTEER	12.95	9.44	7.40
	JAMES MCTEER	12.95	9.44	7.40
	HOUSTON MCTEER	12.95	9.44	7.40
	WILLIAM MCTEER	12.95	9.44	7.40
	ANNIE CUMMMINGS	12.95	9.44	7.40
1/70	ALMEDA CASSON	15.56	11.35	8.88
	ELLA H. HEADRICK	15.56	11.35	8.88
	EDWARD HEADRICK	15.56	11.35	8.88
	MAYNARD HEADRICK	15.56	11.35	8.88
	LUCY HEADRICK	15.56	11.35	8.88
1/84	EDWARD DEAN	12.95	9.44	7.40
	SAMUEL DEAN	12.95	9.44	7.40
	JOHN DEAN	12.95	9.44	7.40
	JAMES DEAN	12.95	9.44	7.40
	WILLIAM DEAN	12.95	9.44	7.40
	KATIE DEAN	12.95	9.44	7.40

Pg. 215 H.C. LANE et ux Vs: OLLIE C. CHANDLER et al. - No. 182
Sold Dec. 14, 1910, to J.A. HEADRICK for $276.00. Distribution:

OLLIE C. CHANDLER	1/5	$34.96
GEORGE CHANDLER		34.96
WILLIE MAY LANE		34.96
LUCILLE CHANDLER	1/10	17.48
ALMA CHANDLER		17.48
WILLIE GREENE	(minor)	34.96
(J.G. GREENE, gdn.)		

LUCILLE and ALMA CHANDLER were minors. Mother - MOLLIE CHANDLER HENDERSON.

Pg. 216 W.P. STEELE et al. Vs: M. HOMER LEE NUCHOLS et al. - No. 162 sold Jan. 22, 1910, to ELIZABETH SIMERLY for $420.00 & W.P. STEELE for $1700.00. Distribution:

JAMES A. STEELE	1/5	$423.70
W.P. STEELE		423.70
B.H. STEELE		423.70
ELIZABETH SIMERLY		423.70
HOMER NUCHOLS	1/15	141.23
BENJAMIN NUCHOLS		141.23
GRACE NELSON NUCHOLS		141.23

Pg. 217 W.H. COLDWELL, admr., Vs: FLOYD HENRY et al. - Bill to sell land for partition and pay debts. Sold Aug. 30, 1910, to W.H. CALDWELL $50.00. Paid bills - No distribution.

Pg. 218 THOMAS N. BROWN, admr., Vs: A.F. BARGER et al. - #176 sold to pay debts. Aug. 20, 1910, lot 9th dist. to HENRY BOYD for $110.00. Aug. 26, 1910, R.B. OLIVER & C.S. GRAVES lot 19th dist. $305.00. Distribution:

A.T. BARGER	1/3	$40.11
BEN BARGER		40.11
ELLA BARGER GARHIRE		40.11

Pg. 220 CHARLES TEFFETELLER et al. Vs: HENRY R. PEDIGO et
& al. - Mar. 1911.
Pg. 224 Distribution: 2nd.Distribution

HENRY PEDIGO 1/5 $189.30
(see order on file Feb. 15, 1911)
MARY A.M. TEFFETELLER   189.30
(see order on file Feb. 15, 1911)
            (E.L. WILKINSON, gdn.)
IZORA E. PEDIGO   189.30 (minor) $171.96
WILLIAM H. PEDIGO   189.30 (minor) $171.96
ANDREW GAMBLE PEDIGO   189.30 (minor) $171.96

Pg. 221 JOHN E. RHEA Vs: J.H. RHEA et al. - #180 sold for debts. Sold Nov. 3, 1910, to J.E. RHEA for $1525.00.
Pg. 223 Distribution: (pg. left blank)

Pg. 225 C.A. TEFFETELLER et ux Vs: SOL SIMERLY et al. - May
1911. Lot sold to R.P. MCREYNOLDS for $203.50. Land
sold to JERRY SIMERLY for $1425.00

Pg. 226 Distribution: 2nd. Distribution
&   SOL SIMERLY 1/9 $93.40 $73.96
Pg. 231 HENRY SIMERLY   93.40   73.96
        JAMES SIMERLY   93.40   73.96
        JERRY SIMERLY   93.40   73.96
        MARGARET NICHOLS   93.40   73.96
        (H. TEFFETELLER)
        JERRY SIMERLY (#3) 1/18   46.70   36.98
        MARGARET TEFFETELLER   46.70   36.98
        MARY TEFFETELLER 1/36   23.35   18.49
        ANNIE TEFFETELLER   23.35   18.49
        NORA SCARBOROUGH   23.35   18.49
        (WILL SCARBOROUGH)
        JOHN NICHOLS   23.35   18.49
        J.H. ROMINES 1/45   18.68   14.79
        GEORGE ROMINES   18.68   14.79
        FRANK ROMINES   18.68   14.79
        MAMIE ROMINES   18.68   14.79
        LULA ROMINES   18.68   14.79
        GEORGE WRIGHT   18.68   14.79
        CHARLES WRIGHT   18.68   14.79
        HUGH WRIGHT   18.68   14.79
        LAURA COKER   18.68   14.79
        (WILL COKER)
        CHARLIE EASLY (EARLY?)   18.68   14.79
        (minor - GEO. WRIGHT, gdn.)

Pg. 228 NEOMA HENRY et al. Vs: INA BELLE GRASTON et al. -
#169 bill to sell filed Apr. 26, 1910. Sold Jul. 26, 1910, to
BRUCE HENRY for $3160.00.

Pg. 229 Distribution: 2nd Distr.   3rd. Distr.
        NEOMA HENRY 1/6 $149.06 $186.08 $191.06
        FRANK GRASTON   149.06   186.08   191.06
        MILTON GRASTON   149.06   186.08   191.06
        JAMES GRASTON   149.06   186.08   191.06
        INA BELLE GRASTON 149.06   186.08   191.06
        (minor)

JENNIE GRASTON   149.06   186.08   191.06
(minor)

Pg. 230 A.M. RULE, admr., Vs: NANCY A. BRADBURN et al. - #190
sold to N.A. BOWMAN for $280.00. Mar. 11, 1911.
Pg. 231 Distribution:
JAMES CHAMBERS   1/3 $29.79
NANCY A. BRADBURN   29.79
LYDIA CHAMBERS   1/18   4.96
IDA CHAMBERS   4.96
A.J. CHAMBERS   4.96
JONNIE CHAMBERS   4.96
ROBERT CHAMBERS   4.96
MAMIE CHAMBERS   4.96

Pg. 233 JOHN A. RUSSELL et al. Vs: ALFRED RUSSELL et al. -
#200 sold Jun. 24, 1911, to J.E. MCCAMPBELL for
$1160.00. Distribution:
CARRIE HEMBREE   1/5 $188.28
GERTIE FRANKLIN   188.28
ALFRED RUSSELL   188.28
RAYMOND RUSSELL   188.28
NELLIE JONES   188.28
(J.A. JONES)

Pg. 234 W.E. BURNER (BARNER?), admr., Vs: PHYLANDER
SINGLETON et al. - #206 sold Jul. 1, 1911, to J.D.
DOCKERY for $285.00. Distribution:
R. PHYLANDER SINGLETON 1/3 $31.57
JOHNIE SINGLETON   1/9   10.52
PEARL SINGLETON   10.52
EMERSON SINGLETON   10.52
ETTA TAYLOR ARMSTRONG   1/6   15.78
JEANE TAYLOR ROBINSON   15.78
(S.C. ROBINSON)

Pg. 235 C.T. CATES, admr., Vs: JOSEPH O. HENRY et al. - #208
sold to JOHN C. CRAWFORD for $120.00. May 27, 1911.
Distribution:
JOSEPH O. HENRY   1/3
GUS HENRY (minor)

ELIZA HENRY
(Only enough funds in above case to pay costs and pre
ferred claims.)

Pg. 237 J.H. MOORE Vs: BLANCH HEADON MOORE. - #216 sold
to GEORGE W. MONROE for $225.00 Feb. 8, 1912. (Court
agrees that J.H. MOORE is the proper person to handle
this money for the benefit of his wife and child. $165.90.)

Pg. 238 J.H. MITCHELL et al. Vs: EDWINA GEORGE. - #214 sold to
C.T. CATE, Jr., for $400.00 Nov. 18, 1911. Distribution:
Mrs. MYRTLE MITCHELL   1/3 $119.20
Mrs. LULA KOPCKE   119.20
EDWINA GEORGE   119.20

Pg. 239 T.C. DOWNEY Vs: ADA C. HENDERSON et al. - #218 sold
Mar. 30, 1912, to T.C. DOWNEY for $200.00. Distribution:
T.C. DOWNEY   1/2 $61.50
            W.P. HENDERSON, gdn.
ADA C. HENDERSON 1/3 of 1/2   (minor)   20.50
GEORGE WM. PATE HENDERSON   (minor)   20.50
JOHNNIE FOUTE HENDERSON   (minor)   20.50

Pg. 240 Mrs. JANE STEELE et al. Vs: ANGIE ARMSTRONG et al. -
#212 sold to W.H. MOORE Dec. 2, 1911, for $406.00. Dis
tribution:
Mrs. JANE STEELE   1/3 $118.46
            W.B. HOWARD, gdn.
ANGIE ARMSTRONG   (minor) 118.46)
RUBY ARMSTRONG   (minor) 118.46)

Pg. 241 JAMES FARMER et al. Vs: DELLA LATHAM. - #224 sold for
partition to J.D MCCLANAHAN for $3725.00. Oct. 1913.

Pg. 242 Distribution:
MARY E. FARMER, widow 1/7 $486.49
JAMES FARMER   486.49
JOE FARMER   486.49
LUNA HENRY "Heirs"   486.49
DELLA LATHAM   486.49
(ED. LATHAM)
GRACE FARMER   (minor)   486.48

(JOE FARMER, gdn.)
NATHAN FARMER   (minor)   486.48
(JOE H. GAMBLE, gdn.)

Pg. 243 JESSIE MCNELLY et al Vs. ESKER MCNALLY. - #234 sold
&   to JOHN BOGLE Nov. 1, 1912, for $2200.00.
Pg. 244 Distribution: 2nd.Distr.:
         ESKER MCNELLY   1/8 of 1 share $139.86 $131.17
         HORACE MCNELLY   139.86   131.17
         HATTIE HOUSTON   (J.O. HOUSTON)   139.86   131.17
         NORA MCNELLY   139.86   131.17
         MAYNEL KELLER   139.86   131.17
         JESSIE MCNELLY   139.86   131.17
                    J.O. HOUSTON, gdn.
         DELMA MCNELLY   (minor)   139.86   131.17
         SANFORD MCNELLY (minor)   139.86   131.17

Pg. 245 J.D. SINGLETON et al. Vs: SAM PORTER et al. - #220 sold
         to J.R. SINGLETON, Jun. 22, 1912, for $7100.00.
Pg. 246 Distribution:
         H.L. MCNUTT heirs entitled to a 1/5 share.
         LOU HITCH   1/9 of a 1/5 share $145.39
         MOLLIE CLARK   145.39
         MARGARET COWAN   145.39
         R.G. MCNUTT   145.39
&   J.A. MCNUTT   145.39
         C.L. MCNUTT   145.39
         ADDIE MCNUTT   145.39
         NORA TEFFETELLER   145.39
         LINA CLARK   145.39
Pg. 268 ELIZABETH SINGLETON heirs entitled to a 1/5 share
         MARY HUMPHREYS   1/5 of 1/5 $261.70
         J.R. SINGLETON   261.70
         MELVINA CLARK   261.70
         J.D. SINGLETON   261.70
         SAM PORTER (dec'd.)   1/4 of 1/5 of 1/5   65.43
&   JENNIE P. TOOLE   65.43
         MAMIE PORTER   65.43
         BOB PORTER   65.43
         WILLIAM MCNUTT heirs a 1/5 share
         BETTY HAMMENS   1/2 of 1/5 $654.26

88

MARGARET GILMER   654.26

Pg. 267 JOHN S. MCNUTT heirs entitled to 1/5 share

MARGARET MCNUTT	1/5 of 1/5	261.70
JENNIE MCNUTT		261.70
Mrs. JAMES F. GRAYSON		261.70
GEORGE MCNUTT	1/6 of 1/5 of 1/5	43.62
ROBERT MCNUTT		43.62
HENRY MCNUTT		43.62
WILLIAM MCNUTT		43.62
MARY L. MCNUTT		43.62
Mrs. WILLIAM GALLENHON		43.62
JOHN B. HUFFORD		43.62
RAYMON HUFFORD		43.62
PAUL HUFFORD		43.62
HAYNES V. HUFFORD	(minor)	43.62
CLOYD HUFFORD	(minor)	43.62
Mrs. JOHN S. DAVIS		43.61

MARGARET PORTER heirs entitled to a 1/5 share

Mrs. M.B. HINES	1/4 of 1/9 of 1/5	36.34
Miss BELL GRAVES		36.34
S. PORTER GRAVES		36.34
Mrs. MOLLIE GRAVES		36.34
Mrs. GERTRUDE MCLIN	1/6 of 1/9 of 1/5	24.23
Mrs. J.P. HOLLER (HELLER?)		24.23
Mrs. A.H. JORDAN		24.23
Mrs. C.M. GALWAY		24.23
Mrs. SOUTHGATE TAYLOR		24.23
Miss J.L. WHITMAN		24.23
Mrs. W.H. BOLING	1/2 of 1/9	72.72
J.M. MCTEER		72.72
Mrs. E.P. GILMER	1/9 of 1/5	145.39
A.L. PORTER		145.39
A.G. PORTER		145.39
Mrs. LAURA NEWBERRY		145.39
S.L. PORTER		145.39
Mrs. IRIS WHITLOCK		145.39

Pg. 248 ELIZABETH M. ALLISON et al. Vs: S.A. JENKINS et al. -
#238 bill to sell land for partition. Sold to G.A. JENKINS
for $551.00. Nov. 1913. Distribution:

S.A. JENKINS	8/10 share	$299.68

ELIZABETH M. ALLISON	1/10	37.46
CORRY THOMPSON	1/6 of 1/10	6.24
COURTNEY THOMPSON		6.24
AUSTIN THOMPSON		6.24
LOUCE THOMPSON		6.24
KATIE THOMPSON FEEZELL		6.25
VIRGIE THOMPSON		6.25

Pg. 249 HESTER BIRDWELL Vs: MARY ANN HAIR, WILLIE BIR-
WELL, JOHN MURPHY EIX, BETTIE ARMSTRONG &
husband, ARMSTRONG. Apr. 1915.
Above case transferred to Chancery Court by Order. Cost of
laying homestead and dower & years support to: Mrs.
SUSAN TAYLOR, wife of A.H. TAYLOR, dec'd.

Pg. 250 R.L. BELK, extr., Vs: GEORGE BREWSTER et al. - #240
Bill to sell land. Sold to BAKER ROY for $230.00 May
1914.

Pg. 251 Distribution:

GEORGE BREWSTER	1/8	$16.29
J.P. BREWSTER		16.29
SARAH BOLINGER		16.29
GEORGIE JENKINS		16.29
(W.B. JENKINS)		
NIECE WELLS		16.29
(WILLIAM W. WELLS)		
THOMAS S. BREWSTER		16.30
DOCK BREWSTER		16.30
ROBERT BREWSTER	(minor)	16.30
(Mrs. ELLA WILLIAMS, gdn.)		

Pg. 252 W.B. CUMMINGS et al. Vs: BILL CUMMINGS et al. - #244
bill to sell land. Sold to J.R. HEADRICK for $3,000.00.
Aug. 1913.

Pg. 253 Distribution:

		2nd.Distrbution:	
BELLE CUMMINGS	1/6	$368.92	$59.61
WILL COULTER		368.92	59.61
JIM COULTER		368.93	59.61
GUY COULTER		368.93	59.61 (minor)
FRANK CUMMINGS	1/2 of 1/6	184.47	29.81 (minor)

AGNES CUMMINGS		184.46	29.81 (minor)
STELLA COULTER	1/6	368.93	59.62

Pg. 254 O.M. LANE Vs: J.E. LANE et al. - #248 sold Aug. 23, 1913, to O.M. LANE for $200.00. Distribution:

O.M. LANE	9/11 of 1/2	$118.50
J.E. LANE	1/11 of 1/2	5.93
MARY MCCALL	1/6 of 1/11 of 1/2	1.00
HARRY RAY		1.00
JOHN RAY		1.00
RONE RAY		1.00
CREED RAY		1.00
MARIE RAY		1.00

Pg. 256 ROSCOE G. COCIIRAN et al. Vs: MASON COCHRAN et al. #228 land sold to STALEY SIMMONS for $15,000.00. Apr. 1913.

Pg. 257 Disbursements:

J.B. COCHRAN heirs

EDNA COCHRAN CURTIS	1/44	$320.81
ALICE BROWN		320.81
PAUL COCHRAN		320.81
ROBERT COCHRAN		320.81
NEOMA COCHRAN		320.81
HATTIE COCHRAN		320.81

JULIA DAVIS heir

ROY DAVIS		320.81

KATE KINNAMON heirs

ROBERT KINNAMON	1/220	64.16
BRICE KINNAMON		64.16
NOLA K. HITCH		64.17
BESSIE K. IRWIN		64.17
SAM KINNAMON, Jr.	(minor)	64.17

J.H. COCHRAN heirs

MASON COCHRAN 1/11 of 1/44 or 1/484		29.17
ROSCOE COCHRAN		29.17
HOMER COCHRAN		29.17
HORACE COCHRAN		29.17
JOHN COCHRAN		29.17
MARTHA COCHRAN (PEERY)		29.17

Pg. 258 ESTHER COCHRAN   29.17

WILL COCHRAN		29.17
THOMAS COCHRAN		29.17
ADA COCHRAN BROWN		29.17
ANN COCHRAN	(minor)	29.17
JOHN COCHRAN, Jr.	1/176	80.20
BERTHA COCHRAN BURTON		80.20
WILLIAM COCHRAN		80.20
CAMPBELL COCHRAN	(minor)	80.20
MARY J. COCHRAN heirs		
ANNIE C. MAU	1/40	160.40
DAISY COCHRAN		160.40
ALEX COCHRAN	1/16	882.24
KENNY COCHRAN		882.24
MARY COCHRAN DEWOOLF		882.24
MARTHA COCHRAN DOWLER		882.24
COLUMBIA COCHRAN WAGLEY 1/20		705.79
NANCY COCHRAN FLEMMING		705.79
ANNIE MAU	1/40	352.89
DAISY COCHRAN	. 1/40	352.90
(on father's side)		

Pg. 277 SAMUEL COCHRAN, dec'd., heirs

TIRZIA ANN RANSON 1/8		1764.49
CALADONIA HUGHS RANSON MCCLINTOCK		1765.49
FLORA C. MCDOWELL, dec'd., heirs		
EXTER MCDOWELL 1/180		78.42
CARL MCDOWELL		78.42
SAMUEL MCDOWELL		78.42
LYNN MCDOWELL		78.42
JULIA MCDOWELL		78.42
ANDRA MCDOWELL		78.42
LIZZIE MCDOWELL		78.42
LORIS MCDOWELL		78.42
FLOSSIE MCDOWELL		78.42

Pg. 278 Disbursements cont'd.

TENNIE L.C. CROWDER, dec'd., heirs	
AGUSTIS CROWDER 1/120	117.63
EDGAR CROWDER	117.63
ALTON CROWDER	117.63
NANNIE CROWDER	117.63
STELLA CROWDER	117.63
SALLIE TINKER	117.63

Pg. 259 GEORGE H. LOWERY Vs: MILLARD RUSSELL, et al. - #__
In county court. Land sold to GEORGE H. LOWERY for
$2535.00 Oct. 1913. Disbursements:
GEORGE LOWERY 5/6 share $1905.10
              NOAH WHITEHEAD, gdn.
MILLARD RUSSELL   1/2 of 1   190.52 (minor)
MARY WHITEHEAD   190.53 (minor)

Pg. 260 A.B. DAVIS et al. Vs: AUDLEY MURR et al. - #252 In
county court. Mar. 1914. Land sold to W.A. GRAVES for
$2610.00.

Pg. 261 Disbursements:
W.L. DAVIS, dec'd., heirs   2nd Disbursement
TISH MILLER   1/11 $99.38 $120.41
A.B. DAVIS   99.38   120.41
SAM DAVIS   99.38   120.41
WILL DAVIS   99.38   120.41
JIM DAVIS   99.38   120.41
GEORGE DAVIS   99.38   120.41
LIZZIE MANIS   99.38   120.41
GRACE DEADRICK   99.38   120.41
  (I.C. DEADRICK)
LUTHER DAVIS   99.38   120.41
KATE FORD   99.38   120.41
  (C.L. Ford)
AUDLEY MURR   1/22 (minor) 49.70   60.25
  (I.C. DEADRICK, gdn.)
LEE FORD   (minor)   49.70   60.24

Pg.263 W.B. HOWARD et al. Vs: BITTLE CRUZE et al. - #226 In
county court. Land sold to W.B. HOWARD for $2100.00.
May 1914.

Pg. 264 Disbursements:
BETTIE CRUZE   1/8 $232.39
W.B. HOWARD   232.40
C.B. HOWARD   232.40
S.S. HOWARD   232.40
JOHN HOWARD   232.40
S.B. HOWARD   1/2 of 1/8   116.20
MAGGIE OUTLAW   116.20
JAMES HENRY   1/5 of 1/8   46.48

93

CORA HUFFSTETLER	46.48	
HORACE HENRY	46.48	
CLEMMIE HENRY	46.48	
ANNIE HENRY	46.48	
MINNIE HYATT	1/4 of 1/5	58.09
LUCY GRIFFITTS	58.09	
ALEXANDER MCCLAIN	58.09	
RUTH LEE HICKS	58.09	

Pg. 265 MARY HILL et al. Vs: CHARLES HILL et al. - #250 In county court. Land sold to Mrs. MARY HILL PHILLIPPS for $150.00. Mar. 1914.

Pg. 266 Disbursements:

MARY HILL PHILLIPS 1/17 share	$2.67	
ED HILL	2.67	
ERNEST HILL	2.67	
GERTRUDE PHILLIPPS	2.67	
CHARLIE HILL	2.67	
JULIA WHIZNANT	2.67	
GREEN HILL	2.67	
ANDERSON HILL	2.67	
LOU OWENS	2.67	
ALICE LANE	2.67	
MARY LEWALEN	2.67	
MARTHA HILL	2.67	
GRACE HILL (minor)	2.67	(MARY HILL
FRED HILL (minor)	2.67	PHILLIPPS
KATIE HILL (minor)	2.67	signed for each
JAMES HILL (minor)	2.67	of these
BEN HILL (minor)	2.67	minors.)

Pg. 269 SARAH J. PHELPS et al. Vs: RICHARD E. PHELPS et al. - #256 in county court sold for partition. Sold to Dr. W.B. LOVINGOOD for $3502.00. Mar. 1914.

Pg. 270 Distribution:

		2nd Disbursement:	
SARAH JANE PHELPS 1/7	$206.86	$265.16	
RHODA ETHEL PHELPS	206.86	265.15	
WILLIAM E. PHELPS 1/7	206.87	265.15	
M.T. BAILEY, gdn.			
RICHARD EARL PHELPS	206.87	265.15	(minor)
V.B. PHELPS	206.87	265.15	(minor)

| VOLA BEATRICE PHELPS | 206.87 | 265.15 | (minor) |
| HENRY VERLAN PHELPS | 206.87 | 265.15 | (minor) |

Pg. 271 JOHN E. ELLIS et al. Vs: WILLIAM L. ELLIS et al. - #260 in county court sold for partition. Mar. 1914. Land sold to J.A. JACKSON, J.L. HACKNEY for $2100.00.

Pg. 272 Disbursements:

JOHN E. ELLIS 1/6 of 1/2	$128.09
WILLIAM L. ELLIS	128.09
LUCY ELLIS HENRY	128.09
CORA M. ELLIS	128.09
FRANK L. ELLIS	128.09
J.L. HACKNEY 1/6 of 1/2	128.09
JOHN E. ELLIS 1/2 of 1/2	469.40
J.L. HACKNEY	469.40

Pg. 273 G.R. OGLE Vs: J.L. OGLE et al. - #266 in county court. Sold for partition. Sold to ED HEADRICK for $1531.00. Apr. 1914.

Pg. 274 Distribution:

J.S. PATTY	3/7 share	$555.33
G.R. OGLE	1/7	185.11
	JOHN S. PATTY, gdn.	
M.T. OGLE	(minor)	185.11
J.L. OGLE	(minor)	185.11
O.A. OGLE	(minor)	185.11

Pg. 275 ROBERT N. MASON Vs: ARTHUR MASON et al. - #268 in county court. Sold for partition / Aug. 1914. Sold to M.F. STEELE for $505.00. Disbursements:

ARTHUR MASON 1/12 share	$34.75	
FRED MASON	34.75	
ORA MASON (STEELE)	34.75	(LAKE STEELE)
ROBERT N. MASON 9/12	312.75	

Pg. 276 JOE H. YOUNCE et al. Vs: THOMAS WALKER et al. In county court of Blount County. Feb. 1915. Disbursements:

| JOE H. YOUNCE 1/2 int. | $12.22 |
| J.R. DUNLAP | 12.22 |

END OF BOOK

EVERYNAME INDEX

----, Edgar 71 Egbert 71 Jas 68
  Jasper 80 Noner 70
ADAMS, Jane 32 Preston 4
  Susan 80
ADMS, Lane 4
AIKEN, Samuel 22
AIKIN, Sam'l 14
ALEXANDER, J D 17 John D 5
  20 Margaret 11 Mary 28
  Samuel 11 W H 46
ALLISON, Blanche Edith 77
  Elizabeth M 89 90 Frank 77
  Lula 70 W S 70
AMERINE, Homer 80 Homer G
  80 R E 58
ANDERSON, A C 10 19 Cather-
  ine 41 E G 41 42 Elizabeth
  67 Flora 41 65 Isaac H 41 42
  J T 72 Lizzie 80 Malinda 3
  Minnie 61 Myra 41 42 R H 3
  R L 41 42 W H 14
ARMSTRONG, Angie 87 Bettie
  90 Etta Taylor 86 John 9
  Nancy R 78 Ruby 87 S M 40
  73 Sarah C 5 W G 40 73 Wm
  A 5
ATCHLEY, Nancy A 58
ATKINSON, M E 57
AUSTIN, Martha 59 Nancy 60
B----, Sam 4

BACON, Sarah 62
BADGETT, Augustine 54 B F 5
  11 Clementine 11 H S 55
  Hettie 54 J N 32 56 78 79
  Mary 55 56 N C 5 R P 56 S H
  55
BADGETTS, Clementine 9
BAILEY, Lucinda 80 M T 94
  Wayne 80
BAKER, Anderson 27 Catherine
  33 James 27 Lucretia 27
  Sallie 27 Samuel 27 Thomas
  27
BARGER, A F 84 A T 84 Ben 84
BARNER, W E 86
BARNHILL, E J 37
BARTLETT, Addison M 45 Clara
  A 45 Cora C 45 Robert A 45
BAYLESS, Alexander 26 Andrew
  V 26 Harrison 26 Mariam A
  26 Sarah H 26
BEALS, Adie 54 E J 57 Eliza-
  beth J 22 I F 4 James F 26
  32 Jas F 22 Sarah A 43
  William 57
BEESON, Amanda 28 Flora 65
  W H 28
BELK, R L 90
BELL, Samuel F 26
BELLUE, Wm 5

97

BENTLEY, Mary 41 66
BEST, Caleb 6 Charles 50 Chris
    2 Chris C 2 Daniel 5 E 5 Earl
    76 Elizabeth 5 20 Elizabeth
    C 5 Elizh A 2 Elsie 76 F R 50
    Fred 24 George 76 Gertrude
    76 J R 75 Jacob 5 6 15
    James M 5 John F 5 20
    Laura 6 15 Louisa 2 Luticia
    48 Lutitia 2 75 M C 2 48 50
    Martha 2 Martha T 6 15 21
    Martin L 6 15 Minnie 76
    Nancy 2 Nancy C 2 R F 48
    Sam'l B 2 Susan 1 2 Tennes-
    see 6 W R 5 20
BEVERLY, Lillie 80
BINGHAM, Annie 49 B I 49
    Hannah L 43 49 James H 49
    Martha 50 Samuel L 43 49
    Thomas D 43 49 Virginia A
    49 W P 49 William 49
BIRDWELL, Hester 90 Willie 90
BLACK, James 5 20 Jas A 17
    Rachel 5 William H 43
BLACKBURN, Lenora 3
BLANKENSHIP, A A 67 E D 2
    Gilbert 2 John 19
BLY, Mary 65 William 65
BOGLE, J C M 14 16-18 55
    John 88
BOLING, W H 89
BOLINGER, Nancy 54 Sarah 90
    W F 24 54
BOREN, Mary 35 Naomi 35
    Tennie 35
BORUFF, A H 75 Sallie 75
BOWERMAN, Fred 80 Perry 80
    S T 32
BOWMAN, Alex 72 Annie 72 N A
    72 86 Nannie 72
BOYD, Elizabeth E 56 Henry 84

BOYD (continued)
    Hugh 44 John M 44 N C 44
    Nannie 81 Roy 44 Sarah J
    44 W A 44 William 44
BRADBURN, Nancy A 86
BRADLEY, 77
BRAKEBILL, Peter 24 W H 16
BREAKBILL, Adam 1 Henry 1
    John 1 Martha J 1 Peter 1
    Salina 1 Serepta 1
BREEDEN, Dialtha 79 Katie 79
    Mary 79 Rebecca 79 Ruth 79
    Sylvester 79
BREWER, Elijah 33 Hetty 33
    Jane 72 John 72 Joseph 72
    M F 51 Martha Ann 80
    Nicholas 33
BREWSTER, Dock 90 George 90
    J P 90 Robert 90 Thomas S
    90
BRIANT, Barbara 6 James 20
    21 Thompson 20
BRICE, S 11
BRIGHT, Arlena 4 Charles 4
    Charly 4 E J 24 Frank 34 G
    A 4 H S 24 Hassie 4 Ida 34
    Julia A 4 Sam B 4
BROADY, Charles F 14 15 Chas
    F 15 J E 25 W C 25
BROWN, Ada Cochran 92 Alice
    91 B S 64 Clifford 63 Cora M
    43 Dexter E 43 E D 42 Ellen
    40 Enoch D 42 George 40 H
    M 67 Hannah S 63 64
    Herman 64 Inez 59 60 J O
    14 Joda 70 John R 42 Kittie
    31 L A 42 Laura 31 M T 42
    Mary 19 Mary A 3 Mary E 31
    Myrtle 64 N J 71 Nellie 70
    Robert 59 Samuel 31 Sandy
    31 Sarah J 14 T N 59 61 69

BROWN (continued)
Thomas 64 Thomas N 45 67
69 84 W P 64 W T 42 William
31
BROYLES, S T 80
BRYANT, Amy E 2 James H 2
John B 2 Joseph T 2 Mary 2
BUNKIS, Lucinda 80
BURN, James W 51
BURNER, W E 86
BURNETT, Florence J 44
BURNS, H J 51 J W 51 James
W 51 John S 81 Lawson 51
W T 51
BURTON, Bertha Cochran 92
BUTLER, Bertie 81
BYERLY, Ernest 70 Frank 70
CALDWELL, Annie B 72 Orzella
83 Phebe 27 R 4 W H 84
CALLAHAN, Lucy 34
CALLOWAY, L L 29
CAMERON, Francis Marion 82
George 82 George M 81 Jane
81 82 John Brooks 82
Mamie B 51 Martha J 51
Minnie B 51 Nancy Alice 82
Roy R 51 William Alexander
82
CANNON, C H 70 Noner 70
CARPENTER, Elisha 13 Horace
63 Margaret 2 Sarah J 13
Samuel 14 T D 26 Thomas
26 W M 63
CARR, Alice 52 Mollie 52
CARROLL, Margaret 53 Martha
81
CARTER, Catherine 62 Katie 79
CARVER, Campbell A 32 Mary E
32
CASSON, Almeda 83
CATE, C T 16 23 C T Jr 87 C T

CATE (continued)
Sr 51
CATES, C T 11 12 40 86 Emma
P 40 J W 40 John C 55 John
W 55
CATLETT, B S 55 Dolly Ann 32
James E 4 Julia J 55 Martha
E 55 Mattie B 55 W H 55
CATTLETT, B S 49
CAUGHRON, E I 74 Elizabeth
Jane 74 W A 68
CAYLOR, Braxton 4 James 66
Jno 3 Martha 66 Perry 4 Wm
T 4
CAYLORE, Betty A 61
CHAMBERLAIN, David 62 Jerry
62 William 62
CHAMBERS, A J 86 Ida 86
James 86 Jonnie 86 Lydia
86 Mamie 86 Prudence 41
Robert 86
CHANDLER, Alma 83 84 George
83 Lucille 83 84 Melissa 34
Ollie C 83
CHAPMAN, Fannie T 69 Ibby 36
CLARK, Eddie 80 Foster 41 J W
A 81 James 15 John 28 Lina
88 Margaret J 15 Melvina 88
Mollie 88 P H 15 Sarah 81
CLARKE, Foster 41 42 65 Foster
Jr 65
CLAYTEN, M C 24
CLEMENS, David 38 61 Eliza 27
Eve 27 Ferdilla 27 H L 27 H
T 38 61 Henry 27 J A 38 62
James M 38 61 Joseph 27 M
E 23 M J 23 Mary 22 Matilda
27 Samuel 27 Samuel R 38
61 Viney 27 W C 22 W E 38
William E 61
CLINE, Jennie 66

COCHRAN, Alex 92 Ann 92
Campbell 92 Daisy 92 Esther
91 Hattie 91 Homer 91
Horace 91 J B 91 J H 76 91
John 91 John Jr 92 Kenny
92 Martha 91 Mary E 41 42
65 Mary J 92 Mason 91
Neoma 91 Paul 91 Robert 91
Roscoe 91 Roscoe G 91
Samuel 92 Thomas 92 Will
92 William 92
COKER, Laura 85 Mary E 37
Will 85
COLDWELL, W H 84
COLLINS, M B 75 Mollie 75
COLTER, Jane 22 Mary E 37 R
R 22
COLUMN, Artie 68 Henry 68
COOK, Eliza 38 Lucinda 2 T W
10
COPELIN, Cordelia F 61
CORT, Nellie E 45
COSTEN, Brice 11 John J 11 20
Martha E 11 Tres Ann 11
COSTNER, Adaline 13 D J 63 H
M 6 15 21 H S 13 John M 6
Margaret 6 Mary 6 Mary J 6
20
COULTER, Andrew 60 Della 72
Guy 90 Jim 90 John M 60
Lora 60 83 Mary C 43 44 S J
52 Stella 91 Will 90
COWAN, J Houston 57 Margaret
88 Mary J 48 Nancy 83 S F
57 Samuel A 57 Samuel F 57
Thomas P 57
COX, Dr 18 Eliza O 59 Henriet-
ta 60 John C 59 Kitty 59
Madison 7 Nathaniel 60
Sallie 83 Sarah 82
CRAWFORD, John C 76 86

CRISP, Charlie 75 Henry 75
Isabella 75 Joe 75 John 75
Mahala 75 Martha 45 Rice
45 Sallie 75 William M 75
CROP, Solithy 27
CROWDER, Agustis 92 Alton 92
Edgar 92 Nannie 92 Stella
92 Tennie L C 92
CRUISE, John 1
CRUZE, Bettie 93 Bittle 93
CRYE, J R 59 Lissie 75 Mary J
34 Melissa 59 Melissa E 59
CULTON, J Wright 53 R C 38 R
L 38
CUMMINGS, Agnes 91 Annie 83
Belle 90 Bill 90 Cora 48
Frank 90 Nancy M 21 Sophia
48 W B 90
CUNNINGHAM, Alfred 4 Ben 28
42 Clay 65 70 Polly 32 Sarah
1
CURTIS, Edna Cochran 91
CUSICK, Rachel 61 S R 56 61
CUTSHAW, Harvey A 71 Harvey
Audley 71 L C 71 Langston
71
DAMMERON, Michael 57
DANIEL, B B 72 Eliza 72 74
DAVID, John 61
DAVIS, A B 61 93 A C 67
Andrew 13 Boyd 77 78 Caleb
F 22 Deeny 75 E 54 Eliz 13
Elizabeth 12 13 Ellen 61 G R
75 G W 22 George 93 George
D 48 Harriet M 48 J F 62 J R
82 Jackson 59 James 12 13
James C 62 James E 22
James R 61 James W 24 Jim
93 Jno V 13 John 13 61
John C 62 John S 21 89
John V 13 Julia 91 Laura C

DAVIS (continued)
    48 Luther 93 Margaret 13
    Margaret J 36 Margaret S 12
    13 Martha F 73 Martin 13
    Mary Ann 36 Mattie 79
    Minerva 13 Nancy 12 13 P T
    33 34 Peter H 22 R C 71 Roy
    91 S L 61 Sadie 61 Sam 93
    Samuel C 48 Sarah 27 62 W
    L 93 W N 21 Will 93 William
    61 William M 46 Wm 13
    Zebulon 71
DEADRICK, Grace 93 I C 93
DEAN, Edward 83 George A 82
    Harry O 82 James 83 Jessie
    82 John 83 Katie 83 Nellie
    82 Samuel 83 Thomas 82
    Walter E 82 William 83
DEARMOND, E C 15 E G 15 J F
    18 J H 15 Jno F 8 John H 8
    18 Margaret 8 R G 15 Susan
    8
DEARMONDS, J H 15 Richard
    15
DELOZIER, J W 56 Jas 56
    Martha E 48 Samantha 38
    Samuel W 56
DENNIS, Elizabeth 42
DEPUTY, Fred 64
DEWOOLF, Mary Cochran 92
DICKERY, David 65
DOCKERY, J D 86
DONALDSON, J H 4 35
DOWLER, Martha Cochran 92
DOWNEY, Caroline 35 T C 87
DRAKE, Margaret 70 71
DRINNEN, James 79 Robert 79
DUNCAN, Harry S 39 Hattie N
    39 James 20 Mary Ann 38
    Mollie M 39
DUNLAP, Barbara 65 J R 94

DUNLAP (continued)
    Lenard 65 Louise E 20
    Martha 65 N E 77 Sara C 22
    William 38 65
DUNN, Daniel 30 Millie 30
DUPES, Lutie 74
DYCHE, J A 9
EAGLETON, D C 15 G F 15 M E
    15
EARLY, Charlie 85 R J 33
EASLY, Charlie 85
EIX, John Murphy 90
ELLIS, Cora M 94 Frank L 94
    John E 94 Mary K 72 Wil-
    liam L 94
ELMORE, Carl H 44 Edgar A 45
    Edith M 45 Fredrick A 45
    Robert B 45
EMERT, Charles 64 Edgar 64
    Edgar S 64 G A 64 W G 64
EMMETT, D W 4
EVERETT, Frank 81 James R
    81 Lem 81 Lucinda 81 Mary
    Ann 27 Rebecca 33
EWING, Mgt 4
FAIN, S A 2 W A 2
FANCHER, Phebe A 51
FARARA, Lillie O 61
FARMER, A 9 Arch 9 Archibald
    9 Bettie J 51 Grace 87
    James 87 Joe 87 88 Lavina
    21 Mary E 87 Mary L 50
    Milley J 9 Nathan 88 Rebec-
    ca 12
FARR, Mary 36 William 36
FEEZELL, Katie Thompson 90
FIELDS, Cyrus 70 Hettie 73
    Hettie A 39 Hetty A 73 Lossie
    70 Lula 70 Margaret 27 Mary
    A C 10
FINLEY, Nancy 62

FLEMMING, Nancy Cochran 92
FLINN, Rebecca 4
FLIPPO, Lou F 53
FORD, C L 93 Kate 93 Lee 93
   Mattie 68
FOWLER, J A 34 Nancy 34
FRANKLIN, Gertie 86
FREEDMAN, R D 72
FRENCH, Andrew 60 C M 60
   Charles 61 Cynthia 8 E P 60
   Elva 60 Flora P 43 Floyd 61
   Homer 60 J B 43 J W 60
   Josh 18 Joshua 8 Lillie 61
   Lucy 60 M 3 Malinda 23 P E
   60 Sarah 60 Walter 60 Wil-
   liam C 43
FRESHOUR, Jacob 46
FROW, 52 Mary H 8 Thomas J 8
   Thos J 18
FRYE, A B 71 Katie 71
FULTON, Ann E 22
GALLENHON, William 89
GALWAY, C M 89
GAMBLE, Andrew 64 Angeline
   12 Angeline F 12 Dora 57
   Hugh 9 J T 71 James T 27
   72 Joe H 76 88 John E 74
   Josias 12 M C 49 51 Malvina
   57 Margaret C 74 Mary 57
   Moses 12 72 Mrs M E 27
   Rebecca 13 S J 74 Sallie 74
   Sam J 74 Sarah J 74
GARDNER, Andrew 37 Bart 36
   George 37 J Bart 37 Jack 36
   James R 37 John 36 Lafay-
   ette 37 Martha 37 Matthew
   36 Nancy 36 Polly 36 Sloan
   37 Susannah 32 T R 32
GARHIRE, Ella Barger 84
GARNER, Eli 13 62 Eliza Jane
   76 Evaline 62 Hugh 62 Hute

GARNER (continued)
   62 J A 43 John R 43 Mar-
   shall 76 Martha 12 13
   Martha Rebecca 77 Matthew
   12 13 Nancy 62 Ransom 77
   Rebecca 12 13 Will 62 Wil-
   liam 24
GEORGE, Barbara 6 21 Barba-
   ra C 7 Edward 6 7 Edwina
   87 Houston 7 21 James
   Edward 6 Kathleen 6 M J 80
   Mary J 6 Mrs Wm 7 R C 6
   Richard 21 S H 6 7 S L 80
   Sam'l L 6
GIBSON, John A 38
GIDEON, Mary 36
GIFFIN, D B 73 74
GILESPY, Will 11
GILLESPIE, C M 4 5 11 J F 11 J
   S 11 James F 4 Jno L 5
   John F 11 John S 4 11 Mrs
   Ann 29 W H 4 5 11
GILLESPY, Ann E 70 Ann Eliza
   69 70 C M 9 11 Hack 70 J H
   51 James F 9 11 John S 9
   11 W H 11 Will 9
GILMER, E P 89 Margaret 89
GODDARD, Lillie 70 W 18 W R
   7 8
GODFREY, John 72 Martha 72
GRAHAM, Pearl J 63
GRANT, Mary 62
GRASTON, Frank 85 Ina Belle
   85 James 85 Jennie 86
   Milton 85
GRAVES, Adam 9 10 13 Bell 89
   C S 84 John A 9 Mahala 9
   Manerva 24 Mira 71 Mollie
   89 S Porter 89 Steven 9
   Steven T 9 W A 93 W Adam
   24 W J 71 W S 76 William

GRAVES (continued)
10 William A 9
GRAYSON, Alabama 31 James F
89
GREENE, J G 83 Willie 83
GREER, 21 David J 9 Elizabeth
63 J A 6-18 22 J J 35 J S 63
J Sherman 57 James A 19
20 James M 9 Joseph C 9
GREGORY, Martha J 71
GRESHAN, 21
GRIBBLE, E 80
GRIFFITH, W V 6
GRIFFITTS, Hester 2 J A 47 J V
47 Lizzie 45 Lucy 94 Phebe
M 47 Ramsey 2 W S 19 W V
34
GRINDSTAFF, W C 31
GUDGER, B M 50
GUY, Catherine 59
HACKNEY, Aaron 21 22 B F 22
David 21 22 Elijah 21 22 J L
22 94 John 21 Levi 22 M B
63
HAFLEY, Caroline 7 8 F W 7 8
Harriett 7 Lutitia 7 S H 8
Samuel C 7 Thomas 7 W C 7
8 W W 8 William 7
HAGGARD, C C 67
HAIR, Mary Ann 90
HALE, Annie 75 P J 50 Samuel
75
HALL, A J 14 Alex 52 E W 41 46
Evelyn 65 F B 41 46 H S 41
46 Hassie 52 Helen 65 J B
41 46 L M 41 46 M E 25
Mary E 41 65 Minnie F 65
Sallie A B 65 W S 25
HAMIL, Hetty 10 Margaret 10
Margaret L 10 Mary J 10 19
Wm F 10

HAMILTON, Elizabeth 52 Lucy
80 William 52
HAMMENS, Betty 88
HAMONTREE, H A 20 J C 31
Mary J 5 Sarah 31
HAMPTON, Alvina 45 Cynthia 6
HANNAH, W A 78
HARBIN, Nannie M 23
HARMON, Annie 83
HARPER, A K 64 80
HASKELL, G W 66
HASSIE, Arlena 4
HATCHER, Anderson 33 E 4 E L
4 Elijah 33 Elijah L 32 Hetty
4 J E 33 34 J W 33 James 4
32 33 Jas 4 Jesse 33 John
32 33 Joseph 4 33 M L 34 N
L 33 Noah 4 32 33 R J 34
Reuban 32 Reuben 4 Rich-
ard 4 33 T W 33 34 Thomas
4 33 William 33 Wm 4
HAWORTH, Eva 43 Wayne L 43
HAYES, J W 6 James A 20
HAYNES, Mary 53
HAYS, Alma 58 Almy 57 James
A 6
HEADRICK, Ami 19 Charles L
82 83 Ed 94 Edward 83 Ella
H 83 Isabella J 43 J A 83 J
H 77 J R 90 James H 83
John H 83 Lena 77 Lucy 83
Martha 27 Maynard 83 P E
82 83 Rhoda 30 W D 69 W F
12 W W 11 William W 83
Wm 4
HEARTSELL, M E 11 W B W 4
HEARTSERL, M E 9
HEATON, Susie 36
HELLER, J P 89
HEMBREE, Carrie 86
HENDERSON, Ada C 87 Edward

HENDERSON (continued)
19 G W 19 George Wm Pate
87 John 19 Johnnie Foute
87 Josiah 19 Lu 65 Mollie
Chandler 84 W P 87
HENRY, Andrew 64 Annie 94
Bruce 85 Clara L J 40
Clemmie 94 Dora 76 Eliza 87
Ellen 61 Eva 63 Floyd 84
Gus 86 H C J 82 Handy 46
Harriet C J 82 Horace 94 J N
43 72 Jacob 25 James 63 93
James S 63 Jane 46 Jerry 23
Joseph O 86 Lucinda 25
Lucy Ellis 94 Luna 87 Mary
A 56 Mary S 63 Neoma 85
Ongus 76 Pleasant 28 72
Riley 46 Robert 40 S W 28 W
L 28 Wm 2
HENSLY, Mary P 38
HICKS, Carl 70 Elizabeth 34 35
70 Ernest 70 Grace 70
James 70 Ruth Lee 94
HILL, Anderson 94 Ben 94
Charles 94 Charlie 94 Ed 94
Ernest 94 Fred 94 Grace 94
Green 94 James 94 Katie 94
M A 33 34 Martha 94 Mary
94
HINES, Florence J 44 Harvey Ed
44 James H 44 Lee A 44 M B
89 Mary H 44 Nellie R 44
Stella M 44
HINTON, Dorcas 23 S C 6 14 17
19 23
HITCH, E 74 J A 48 James A 48
Lou 88 Nola K 91 Rachel 61
HOBBS, Margaret 56 Sarah 53
HOLLAND, Effie 49 James 35
Mary D 29 Myrtle 49 Nora
Bell 49 Sarah E 29 35 48

HOLLAND (continued)
Sarah J 49
HOLLER, J P 89
HOOD, Annie E 54 Grace L 58
Lucas 7 21 Margaret E 58 R
N 17 20 W P 58
HOPPER, Mary 79 80
HOUSTON, Hattie 88 J O 88 M
A 43 R L 43
HOWARD, C B 93 Eliza J 10 H
P 45 J C 28 J E 43 John 93
John R 10 S B 93 S S 24 93
W B 10 81 87 93
HOYL, Mary M 39 Mary N 73
Samuel T 39
HUDGEONS, Eliza 28 J J 4 28
HUFFORD, Cloyd 89 Haynes V
89 John B 89 Paul 89
Raymon 89
HUFFSTETLER, Cassie 75 Cora
94 Dora 75 Florence 63 John
D 75 M A 75 Robert 75 Will
75
HUGHES, M E 33 34
HUMPHREYS, M E 4 Mary 88
HUNPHREYS, Wm C 4
HUNT, I T 68 James 4 S E 68
HUNTER, A C 1 Samuel 1
Samuel M 1 Thomas 1
HUSKEY, Alexander 51 Arthur
51 Lucy 51
HUTSELL, Frank 75 Jeff 66 Lee
66 Los 66 Martha 66 Mel 66
Mollie 66 Sarah 75
HUTTON, Alabama 31 Elizabeth
2 N C 54
HYATT, Minnie 94
IRWIN, Bessie K 91 Jane 68
Jesse T 12
ISH, Frank 30 Letitia 29 30
JACKSON, Elizabeth 33 Ellen

JACKSON (continued)
60 J A 94 Mary Ann 33
JAMES, Dorcas 27 Jesse R 32
John J 11
JEFFERIES, Bertha 67 Cather-
ine C 45 H J 45 Harvey 45
James 45 James H 45 John
67 John E 45 May 67 Rebec-
ca 67 Susan A 67 Susan
Ann 67 William Alfred 67
JENKINS, G A 89 Georgie 90 J
B 34 Kate 41 S A 89 W B 90
JOHNSON, 57 Amanda M 49
Charles E 37 Chas E 37
George L 49 H L W 26 H W L
26 James A 37 John M 37
Mallie F 49 Mariah 26
Martha 37 Mary C 37 Nina
37 O P 37 Oliver P 37 R C 37
Richard H 26 27 Sarah J 44
Thomas C 56 Thomas M 27
W H 37 William J 60
JONES, E A 58 E D 29 Eliza-
beth 19 Harlin C 11 J A 86
John H 11 John W 11 20
Mary M 44 Nellie 86 S L 58
Tres Ann 11
JORDAN, A H 89
KAGLEY, Betsy Ann 37 Charley
74 Evelinda 32 Florence 74
Francis 74 Ida 74 J A 31
Lenard 74 Margaret 37
Nancy J 31 T A 74 Z A 32
KAISER, Anna 40
KEEBLE, Bettie J 49 C G 76 E
G 48 50 Ed 77 Ed G 50
Hugh L 76 James 77 James
E 76 John E 48 50 John R
76 Lutitia 76 M A 49 50 M C
48 M E 50 M L 48 50 M P 48
50 Marion P 50 Martha A 50

KEEBLE (continued)
Matilda C 50 Maud 77 R P
48 49 51 S G 49 50 Sam W
77 Sine G 50
KEENE, Gilbert 3 Gilbert P 3
James 3 M H 3 Thursey M 3
William 3
KELLAR, A B 69 Betsy 69 71 G
W 31 Issac T 69 James L 32
John H 32 Joseph W 31
Nancy 69 Robert B 32
KELLER, Andrew 36 Elizabeth
36 G W 31 George K 23 Isaac
36 J H 31 J L 23 31 J T 32
58 J W 31 Joseph W 31 L E
23 M E 23 M J 23 Maynel 88
Nancy 36 Phebe J 23 Phro-
nia 36 Samuel 32 W H 22
KELLY, Jane L O 38
KENNEDY, A 9 Alex 9 C M 66
Mary A 66
KERR, Betsy 37 Charles 31
Clabo 31 Daisy M 31 David
31 37 Dolly 37 Elizabeth 24
Gin 31 James 24 James B
31 Jesse 31 John 24 31
Martha E 31 Nancy 24 Polly
Ann 2 R M 31 William 31
KEY, Charles 53 Connie 72
Dawson 53 Dora 53 Mary R
39
KIDD, Adda 23 Blanche Edith
77 Bruce M 72 Charles A 77
Charles J 23 Charley A 76
Della M 73 E F 55 Edgar F
73 Emma 23 Ferada Lindsay
77 Frances 72 H G 76
Horace G 77 L M 55 Lowry R
76 77 Margaret 23 O C 55
Robert P 72 Sarah J 56
KING, James M 23 Sarah Susan

KING (continued)
82
KINNAMON, Ann E 44 Brice 91
Kate 91 Robert 91 Sam 91
KINNICK, J T 78 82
KIRBY, G W 79 George W 79 J L
79 Sarah 34
KITRELL, Belle 68
KITTRELL, Robert 68
KIZER, Annie 75 G D 29 Ida 82
Mollie 75 Oscar 75 S H 75
KOPCKE, Lula 87
LACKEY, John W 19
LAMBERT, Cornelia B 53
LAMON, David 2 3 George 67
James 3 Joseph 2
LANE, Alice 94 Charles M 25
Cicero R 25 Eliza 2 Eliza J
25 H C 83 J E 91 James L
25 John 81 John R 25 Lula
81 M E 26 Maggie A 25
Malinda E 25 Martha A 25
Mary E 24 O M 91 Rachel 27
S D 26 Serbern 45 Tennie 75
W A 25 William A 24 Willie
May 83
LANGSTON, Benjamin 45
LARGE, John 32 Sarah 42
LATHAM, Della 87 Ed 87 Edd
71 Egg 71 Lester 71 Walter
71
LAW, Abraham 73 Elizabeth 73
H G 73 77 H Leonard 73 77
Henry C 80 J L 73 J O 73 J
T 73 77 Jackson O 73 Jas T
77 Jimmie 73 John 24 Lizzie
77 Martha 27 Rachel 61
Rebecca 73 W A 73 Wesley
73 Willie 77
LAWRENCE, J S 7 Kathleen 7
LAWSON, D B 30 Ella 72 Ellen

LAWSON (continued)
72 74 J D 30 J L 30 J W 30
T J 30 72 W H 30
LEATHERWOOD, George 42
John 42 Joseph 42 Thomas
42 W L 42
LEDFORD, Harriet M 38
LEE, Edwin 51 Ezra H 35
Florence Ann 51 George Jr
51 John R 3 L R 43 Lewis 51
T R 21 43
LENG, Mary E 32
LESTER, Anna 31
LEWALEN, Mary 94
LEWIS, W J 78
LINDLEY, Milton 21 Sophorona
P 21 Sophrona P 22
LINE, Henry 49 63
LIPSCOMB, Minerva 16 Wm Ira
16
LOGAN, Alex W 21 Alexander 1
Charles 67 Elizabeth 67
Flora E 24 Hugh L 21 James
W 24 John 67 John H 21
Lucinda 24 Martha M 21
Mary J 21 Narcissa 21 Sam
67 Samantha 78 Samuel 19
67 W A 68 70 78
LONG, A R 23 Alford 74 Alfred
74 C J 23 Frank 27 George
27 George C 74 Jacob T 74
James 27 John H 74 Joseph
74 Lou 66 Mary 27 Minnie
70 Sally 74 W H 74 William
27
LOVE, C R 64
LOVINGOOD, W B 94
LOWE, Deeny 75 Linn Ann 75
LOWERY, George 93 George H
93
LUSTER, W W 3 6

106

MALCOLM, J W 2 Jane 2 Jno 2
MALCOM, Alice 14 Emma 14
   John E 14 Phoebe 14
   Samuel 14 W B 14
MALCUM, Alice 22 Emma 22
   John E 22 Phebe 22 Samuel
   22
MANIS, Lizzie 93
MAPLES, Rebecca 33
MARANVILLE, Riley 20
MARSHALL, L V 25 M J 25
MARTIN, D K 2 Frances 42
   Hugh 42 J H 43 James H 24
   42 John 43 John H 5 Joseph
   H 42 Julia 42 Mary E 43
   Rossie J 43 Sallie C 5
   Samuel 42 W G 24 William
   42
MASON, Arthur 94 Fred 94 Ora
   94 Robert N 94
MATHES, Littleton 2 Mary 2
MATLOCK, Barbara 7 Barbara
   C 7 Bessie 72 John 72 Mack
   72 Margaret 19 W R 7
MATTHEWS, James 20
MAU, Annie 92 Annie C 92
MAYS, James 1
MCADAMS, Chambers 9
MCADONY, Chambers 11 12
MCAMPBELL, Samuel 65
MCBATH, W O 50
MCCALL, Hettie 79 Mary 91
MCCAMPBELL, Benjamin 41
   Benjamin B 65 Bruce 41 66
   Charles 41 66 Houston 66 J
   E 86 J H 46 James 41 65 66
   James M 41 Jane 41 John
   41 66 John Mccormack 41
   Leonidas 41 66 Mary B 65
   Sallie A B 65 Samuel S 41
   William 41 66

MCCAMY, Elizabeth 53 James
   53 62 John 62 L F 12 Louisa
   12 Martha E 62 Matilda A 38
   Nola 62 R A 12 Sarah 62
   William 53
MCCASLAND, James 3 Jerry 3
   Jno 3 John H 3 Mary 3
   Sydia A 3 William 3 Wm 3
MCCINLE, W D 16
MCCINLEY, W D 19
MCCLAIN, A 19 Alexander 94
MCCLANAHAN, J D 87 M E 37
   M L 63 Margaret 62 Martha
   62 Rachel 12 13 Wm S 13
MCCLINTOCK, Caladonia
   Hughes Ranson 92
MCCLUNG, John Earnest 30
   Nannie B 30
MCCLURES, Edith 22
MCCLURG, Joseph F 44
MCCOLLUM, Dolly 5 J B 31
   Nancy 31
MCCONNELL, Betsy Ann 82 J H
   10 17 Jno N 14 John 14
   John M 22 John N 14 Mary
   10 Mary A 17 W L 82
MCCOY, David X 38 George 38
   Margerry E 38 Nancy 38
   Robert B 38 William M 38
MCCULLEY, Ida J 44 Ida Jane
   44
MCCULLOCH, Andrew E 56
   Cora E 56 Estella A 56 Grace
   A 48 56 Hetty 54 Hetty C 54
   Hugh Emma 56 John A 56
   John C 48 56 John D 56
   Lennie 56 S J 54 Samuel W
   48 56
MCCULLY, Matilda H 45
MCDOWELL, Andra 92 Carl 92
   Exter 92 Flora C 92 Flossie

MCDOWELL (continued)
92 Julia 92 Lizzie 92 Loris
92 Lynn 92 Samuel 92
MCFADDEN, J S 69 Mrs J M 27
MCGHEE, Alexander 3 Eliza-
beth 6 Jas 6
MCGINLEY, Annie 83 L 27
MCILVAINE, J 74 Joe 74 Joseph
I 68
MCINLEY, W D 12
MCINTURFF, Hester 75
MCKENRY, Dorcas 21 Samuel
21
MCKENZIE, J C 23
MCLIN, Gertrude 89
MCMAHON, Elizabeth 1
MCMILLAN, J S 81 Margaret J
81
MCMURRY, Margaret 19 Wil-
liam 19
MCNAB, John 10
MCNABB, A T 10 17 C P 71
Charles Gamble 72 J H 10
11 James H 10 17 James N
10 Jas H 17 Jno 17 John 10
John N 10 17 Paul Edgar 72
MCNABBS, Jno 10
MCNALLY, Esker 88
MCNELLY, Delma 88 Esker 88
Horace 88 Jessie 88 Nora 88
Sanford 88
MCNUTT, Addie 88 C L 88
Frankie 57 George 89 H L 88
Henry 89 Irene 57 J A 80 88
Jennie 89 John S 89 Marga-
ret 89 Mary L 89 Nellie 57 R
G 88 Robert 89 William 88
89
MCREYNOLDS, Cora 77 John G
44 R P 29 30 44 49 54 79 80
85 Robert P 44 Sarah T 44

MCREYNOLDS (continued)
William M 44
MCTEEER, James 83
MCTEER, Alex B 37 Alexander
B 37 Andrew B 29 Anna C
60 Houston 83 J M 89
James E 60 John 83 John H
60 Mrs Nancy 29 Nancy 29
Ruth J 46 S B 82 Samuel H
60 Samuel Houston 60 Will
A 29 51 Will M 60 William 83
William L 60
MEAD, Fannie H 29
MEADOWS, Tennessee 62
MEANS, Charles S 39 Chas S
39 Cora A 39 Jno N 2 Mary
V 39 Minnie G 39
MILLER, Albert 55 Anderson 55
Annetta 55 D B 55 Dorthula
55 Emma 75 Georgia 41 46
Ida H 55 J D 78 J H 55 J L
55 M L 55 Marshall 55 Mary
55 O L 75 R B 55 Sarah J 55
T J 55 Tish 93
MILLS, Hester 8
MILLSAPS, Elizabeth 4 32 33 J
E 4
MILSAPS, Bud 81 Jasper 80
Kitty 81 Mart 81 Mike 81
Nancy 81 P W 80 81
MISER, G M D 48
MITCHELL, J H 87 Mary B 41
65 Myrtle 87
MONROE, George W 87
MONTGOMERY, A B 29 A C 16
E C 29 E M 25 E R 25 Flora
A 29 G W 25 65 78 H A 16
Hettie 16 Hetty A 26 J E 29
John 25 John E 29 Kittie 31
L G 25 M J 23 M M 78
Maggie 31 Maggie A 25

MONTGOMERY (continued)
Margaret A 25 P G 16 R G 29
R M 16 Robert 31 S C 25 S O
29 Samuel 16 26 W G 23 25
MOON, James A 35 Sarah A 35
MOONEY, Mary 59
MOORE, Blanch Headon 87 J B
39 J H 87 James A 39 53
John W 39 53 Joseph B 39
53 Priscilla 60 W H 87
MORRIS, Florence 52
MORRISON, Charles 65 George
64 James 64 Jennie E 39
Mary 64 Robert 64 65
MORTON, George M 48 H H 2
Ida C 48 J G 54 Jennie H 48
Jesse Ann 48 Mary L 48
Rebecca J 48
MOSIER, G L 49 M E 50 Sarah
50
MULTS, Hattie 80
MURDOCK, Eliz J 59 Elizabeth
J 60
MURPHY, Clara 54 Martha J 83
W C 12
MURR, Alexander 69 Audley 93
Jane 36 69 M N 23 Mary
Jane 69 Tilda 23
MURRIN, Catherine 58 John 58
Joseph 58 Mariah 58 Mary A
58 Mary Ann 58 Nancy E 58
Rachel 58 Robert 58 W M 58
William 58
MYERS, Henry 81
NELSON, Mary C 20
NEWBERRY, Laura 89
NEWBERT, Rachel 72
NEWMAN, Elizabeth 1
NICHOLS, John 85 Margaret 85
NICHOLSON, Maggie 42 66
NORTON, G 56 John 48 Magno

NORTON (continued)
lia 48 Martha E 56
NUCHOLS, Ben 76 Benjamin 84
Elijah 26 Grace 76 Grace
Nelson 84 Homer 76 84
Homer Lee 84 Jane Alexan-
der 57 John 26 Mary J 25 N
F 25 R A 61 S L 62 63 Sarah
J 61 W M 61 70 76 77
NUN, E 12 Martha L 18 Nancy
18
NUNS, Nancy 8 Nancy J 8
OAR, Margaret 11
OGLE, G R 94 Henry H 45 J L
94 M T 94 O A 94
OLIVER, Mary 30 R B 84 Wil-
liam H 30
ONEAL, Nancy 34
ORR, 17 Malcena 67 Martha 42
OUTLAW, Maggie 93
OWENS, Lou 94
PALMER, James 1
PARHAM, Charles L 40 Edward
F 40 Guy H 40 R A 40 W E
40 W T 40
PARKER, David 45 Harris 73
Lee 73 Margaret 45
PARKINS, Jane 45
PARKS, Abner 63
PARROT, Mary 42
PARSONS, A L 17 H A 17 J C 17
J K 17 John C 49 Mary E 49
PASCHAL, Lillian 57
PASCHEL, Lillian 58
PATE, Mary 59
PATTY, J S 94
PAYNE, Phebe A 32
PEARSON, Ralph 3
PECK, H L 66 Hannah 41 J P 66
PEDIGO, Andrew Gamble 84
Henry 84 Henry R 61 84

PEDIGO (continued)
Henry Robert 58 Isabella J
57 Izora E 84 Izora Elizabeth
58 Mary Anna 58 William H
84 William Hobart 58
PETERS, J F 63 J L 63 N C 63
PFLANZE, C 49
PHELPS, Charlie 79 Clestia 55
Ella 55 Henry Verlan 94 Ina
79 J G 79 J S 79 John C 54
55 Oliver 79 Pearl 79 Rhoda
Ethel 94 Richard E 94
Richard Earl 94 Robert 79
Sarah J 94 Sarah Jane 94
Sarah Saline 54 55 V B 94
Vola Beatrice 94 Walter 79
William E 94
PHIFER, 57 Richard 56 Robert
56 W C 56 Will C 56
PHILLIPPS, Gertrude 94 Mary
Hill 94
PHILLIPS, Mary Hill 94
PICKENS, Elizabeth 54 Geneva
56 Hetty 53 J A 54 J P 54
John P 54
PITNER, Mary J 60
PLEMONS, Margaret 27
PORTER, A G 89 A L 89 Bob 88
E E 16 Evaline E 16 Mamie
88 Margaret 89 P J 16
Phoebe J 16 S L 89 Sam 88
W H 16
POTTER, Sophronia 69
PROFFITT, Addie E 72
QUEENER, T W Jr 49
RANKIN, J H 32 Milton 32
RANSON, Tirzia Ann 92
RASAR, Charles 36 Lee 36
RATLEDGE, Daniel 64 J T 67
Lizzie 64 William 67 Wright
67

RAULSTON, Anna 44 J P 10 W
H 10
RAY, Creed 91 Harry 91 John
91 Marie 91 Obadiah 28
Rone 91
REEBLE, C G 76 Docie Don 76
W Thomas 76
REONES, Hetty 33
RHAY, Ambrose 28 Sarah 28
Virginia 28
RHEA, J H 84 John E 69 84
John P 35
RHYNE, Evaline H 27
RIMER, Cynthia R 15 M A 15
RING, Mary R 28
ROBERTS, Joseph 65
ROBERTSON, H L 63
ROBESON, C D 34 Martha E 34
Mary 34
ROBINSON, Jeane Taylor 86 S
C 86
RODDY, M A 30 William 20
RODGERS, Mary 57 58 Will 57
William 57 Willie 57 58
ROGER, W B 63
ROGERS, A J 63 Emily 21 J H
20 Jesse 9 John V 63 L W 63
Martha 9 20 Mary 62 Mary A
32 W B 63
ROMINE, Charles 81
ROMINES, Frank 85 George 85
J H 85 Lula 85 Mamie 85
RORAX, Caroline 2 John 2
ROREX, Absalom 52 Andrew Jr
51 Frank 52 George 52
Hiram 51 52 Luella 52
Maggie 52 Noga 6 7 Sam 7
ROSE, Edward W 51 Hammie L
51 Roy N 51 Sarah R 51
ROSS, G B 14 G W 73 John 73
Lanty M 73 M T 39 N P 14

ROSS (continued)
Nancy 14 Nancy J 22 S A 26
Sam T 73
ROWAN, Sam P 11 16
ROY, Baker 90
RULE, A M 55 86
RUSSELL, Alfred 86 E J 21
Elbert 43 H H 73 Isaac 21
John A 86 John L 19 M L 29
Millard 93 Raymond 86 Ruth
43 Sarah 16 T D 64 W L 29
RUTLEDGE, Delia 16 George C
16 Minerva 16
RUTTER, Jennifer 13
SAFFELL, E A 26 J T 26
SANDS, Catherine 82
SCARBOROUGH, Nora 85 Will
85
SCOTT, Andrew 82 Iowa 77
John P 25 Lucinda 25 Sarah
M 34 Sherman 82 W B 25 W
H 77
SCROGGS, Bleunt L 26 Bruce F
26 Horace M 26 John M 26
Julia M 26 Mary E 26
Thomas B 26
SEATON, Mary 72
SELLARS, Edwin 40 Ira 40
Jophata 40 May 40
SELLERS, Edwin 40
SHADDAN, John H 39
SHANE, J H 65
SHARP, Ida 79
SHAVER, Fate 53 Freeling 53 H
C 53 54 J H 7 J Houston 53
James H 7 Jesse 53 John 53
Lewis 54 Mary 54 Pearl 54
Viney 26 W E 53 William 26
53
SHERRILL, Rachel 61
SHIELDS, A J 64 Andrew J 64

SHIELDS (continued)
Elijah 29 Flora E 64 James F
64 John E 64 Mary E 64
Mary J 64 Olie Z 64 Rachel
64 William H 64 Zachariah
64
SHULER, H T 78
SIMERLY, Elizabeth 84 Henry
85 James 85 Jerry 85 Sarah
Sr 67 Sol 85
SIMMONS, C N 44 Martha E 32
Staley 91
SIMPSON, Martha 41 66
SINCLAIR, A W 24 Flora E 24
SINGLETON, Elizabeth 88
Emerson 86 J D 88 J R 88
Johnie 86 Pearl 86 Phyland-
er 86 R Phylander 86
SLEMONS, Ellis 59
SLOAN, William 2
SMITH, Clyde 59 Mamie Cox 60
Martha 42 66 W G 59
SNELSEN, H J 32
SNIDER, Dave E 8 James 8
James L 8 Susan 8
SPARKS, Alfred 47 Bertie 78 D
W 82 David W 47 Ed 47 52
Eliza J 44 Emeline 47
George H 47 J T 47 52
James 78 James A 47 52
Jane 78 Jereme 78 John T
47 Julia A 78 Lucy 78
Margaret L 52 Margaret Lee
47 Martha E 53 Martha
Emeline 47 Mary Louise 82
May 78 N E 52 N H 44
Samuel L 47 Samuel N 47 52
78 William 47 Willie 47 53
SPEARS, Mary Jane 63
SPILLMAN, Fletcher 38 Marian
38

SPRINGFIELD, Alice 22
SPURGEON, Pheobe J 65
STAFFORD, Adam 81 Calvin 80
81 James 81 Lucy Ann 81
STEELE, B H 84 James A 84
Jane 87 Lake 94 M F 94 Ora
94 W P 84
STEINER, Roena 66
STEPHENS, Betsey 27 David 23
J C 23 Mollie 74 R A 23 35
Richard 23 Samuel 22 23
Sarah E 36 Sarina 74 W R
23
STEPHENSEN, Lizzie J 52
Martha A 52 William G 52
STEPHENSON, Margaret E 47
STEWART, G L 49
STINNETT, Eliza 6
STONE, Sarah 32
STOUT, Rebecca 33 Rebecca
Ann 33 Susanna 68
SWAGGERTY, Dela 75 Mahala
75
SWANEY, James 20
TALLENT, A M 37 Avery 53
Benjamin 38 Bettie 37 C B
39 D E 39 Delia 53 J E 39
James 38 53 Jeannette 53
John 53 John W 39 L A 39
Leuiza J 39 Mary J 39
Samuel A 53 Sula 37 W A 39
TALLY, Isabella 38
TAYLOR, A H 90 A J 62 Ben 1 2
C G 70 Calvin 59 Catherine
54 Charles 35 60 Charles M
59 Cornelia 59 D R 70
Daniel 59 Elizabeth 1 Eliza-
beth J 59 G H 69 70 George
35 H O 34 I W 54 Isaac 2 30
James 1 2 34 54 James C 59
James G 59 Jo Anna 35

TAYLOR (continued)
Joanna C 59 Lafayette 59
Lycurgus 59 Margaret 2
Mary 1 2 Milton C 60 Mollie
35 Nancy 2 30 60 R F 59
Redden G 60 Richard 35
Robert 59 Rufus F 59
Samuel R 59 Southgate 89
Susan 1 2 90 Susannah 34
W A 70 William 2 34 35
William L 59
TEDFORD, Baxter 40 Eliza 41
Ewell 40 J H 40 John H 41
M J 59 Martha 59 Mary 73
74 Oscar 41 R A 40 R H 40
W D 41
TEFFETELLER, Alford 66 Annie
66 85 C A 85 Calvin 35
Charles 84 Clarence 66
Evaline 35 H 85 Mary 85
Mary A M 84 Nora 88 Wil-
liam 66
THOMAS, Frances E 42 John 78
THOMPSON, A B 31 32 Andrew
36 Andrew B 36 67 69 71
Austin 90 Benjamin 69
Campbell 5 17 Charles 69
Corry 90 Courtney 90 David
36 David C 30 E T 5 G W 31
George 35 36 67 69 71 Hil-
larde J 5 J E 30 Jack 36
James 35 36 James B 36
Jane 35 Jno P 17 John 5 35
36 John Andrew 69 John H
30 36 69 Katie 69 71 L W 30
Laura 12 Lon 12 Louce 90
Margaret 35 Martha A 17
Martha E 31 Martin 35
Mattie 69 Millard B 5 Naomi
30 R A 30 Robert 36 Robert
A 30 Robert H 30 Samuel 36

THOMPSON (continued)
Sarah S 32 Thomas 35 36
Virgie 90 W H 30 W W 30
Wells 5 Will F 71 William 36
69 71
TILLERY, Bettie A 7 Jane 7 8 W
T 8
TINKER, Sallie 92
TIPTON, Dorcus 24 J Harten 24
J Horton 24 Jacob 24 John
A 24 M E 29 Peter 24
TOOLE, Jennie P 88 M A H 9 N
E 5 R O 5 W A H 9 W P 5 9
11 William 5 Wm 5
TOOLES, M A 11
TRICE, Nancy J 20 W R 20
William 20
TROTTER, 4
TRUNDLE, 57 Anna 56 Clemmie
56 Ella 56 Leatha 56 Ophelia
56
TRUSLOVE, Maud Austin 60
TUCK, Edward 3 6 34 Henry 3 6
J M 3 Jackson 3 6 Louise 68
Mary 6 Mary J 3 Samuel 68
Sebe 68
TUCKER, R C 4
TUCKERS, R C 20
TULLOCH, C B 39 E M 10 Eva
M 10 George H 10 James 10
James C 10 John C 39 John
M 10 Mary A C 10 W H 10
Wm H 10
TURLEY, Catherine 59
VAUGHT, Jackson 28 Richard
28 Sarah 28 William 28
WAGLEY, Columbia Cochran 92
WALKER, 4 James A 54 Joseph
L 3 Mary E 26 P F 28 Spen-
cer 26 Thomas 94 V B 50
Wm 3

WALLACE, A H 68 Charles E 28
Charlotte 52 Georgia 81 J L
14 J Lamar 14 15 John A 81
Leota 81 Louisa 28 Nancy J
14 15 Nora 81 Ora 81 Pearl
G 49 Peggy Jane 68 Sue 81
W P 55
WALLER, E B 64
WARD, Bessie 69 Burgess C 69
Ella May 77 78 George 68
James 68 Jesse 68 John 68
Nettie 68 Newton 68 R J 68
S C 68 Susie 69 William 68
70 Wm 68
WARREN, M B 29
WATERS, Elizabeth 51 Houston
70 71 J H 71 John 70
Johnnie 71
WEAGLY, Mrs Clara 29
WEAR, Elizabeth 67 Elizabeth A
67 Martha 47 52
WEBB, Henry 3 Robt L 3
WEBBS, Nancy C 7
WELCKER, Albert 30 Dixie 30
Henry 30
WELLS, B C 54 Henry A 54 J D
54 John B 77 John S 54
Niece 90 William W 90
WEST, Burgess 69 70 Della 69
70 George 69 70 H A 5
Harriett J 5 N R 5 Payton 70
Sam 69 70
WHEELER, Sally 38
WHITE, John Alfred 46
WHITEHEAD, Elizabeth J 71
Frank 79 George W 62 J
Calvin 62 J J 62 Jennie 79
John 62 Margaret 62 63
Mary 93 Mary Ellen 79 Noah
93 Peggy 36 Porter 62 Wil-
liam 78 William A 62 Wil

WHITEHEAD (continued)
   liam T 79
WHITLOCK, Iris 89
WHITMAN, J L 89
WHITTEN, Dorthula 50
WHIZNANT, Julia 94
WILCOXEN, Jane E 29
WILKINSON, E L 84
WILLARD, 3 Earnest 53 Fred 53
WILLIAM, L C 2
WILLIAMS, A T 25 Addie 69 Ella
   90 J H 57 J M 57 J M Jr 57
   J W 43 Lula N 57 58 M G 25
   Sarah E 50 W D 57 W M 2
WILLIAMSON, Horace E 43
WILLIS, Susan C 48
WILLOCKS, Martha 37
WILLS, B C 54 Henry A 54
WILSON, Annie M 40 Golde 3 H
   I 9 H M 65 Mary 42 R I 8 16
   Rachel 42 William 38

WINTON, Galddis 80 Georgia 80
   Helen 80 Smith 80
WOLF, Martha 53
WOODFIN, Colville M 16 J F 16
   17 Jno S 16 John S 16 Juliet
   16
WOODS, C A 50 Dorcan 24
   Samuel 50
WOOLSEY, Eliza 34 Martha E
   34
WRIGHT, Charles 85 Geo 85
   George 85 Hugh 85 Millie 68
   W H 28 29
YEAROUT, I R 52 Isabella I 52 J
   M 52 Jno M 52 N R 52 Ruth
   B 39 S N 52 Samuel N 52
YOUNCE, Joe H 94
YOUNG, Adella 50 Isabella 67 J
   E 76 John 50
ZACKERY, Emma 22